Leadership
Mastery
in Turbulent Times

HERB KINDLER, PH.D.

With Contributions By
Marlene Caroselli, Ed.D.

THOMSON
━━━━━━━━━━✳━━━━━━━━━━™
COURSE TECHNOLOGY
Professional ■ Technical ■ Reference

Important: Thomson Course Technology PTR cannot provide software support. Please contact the appropriate software manufacturer's technical support line or Web site for assistance.

Thomson Course Technology PTR and the author have attempted throughout this book to distinguish proprietary trademarks from descriptive terms by following the capitalization style used by the manufacturer.

Information contained in this book has been obtained by Thomson Course Technology PTR from sources believed to be reliable. However, because of the possibility of human or mechanical error by our sources, Thomson Course Technology PTR, or others, the Publisher does not guarantee the accuracy, adequacy, or completeness of any information and is not responsible for any errors or omissions or the results obtained from use of such information. Readers should be particularly aware of the fact that the Internet is an ever-changing entity. Some facts may have changed since this book went to press.

Educational facilities, companies, and organizations interested in multiple copies or licensing of this book should contact the publisher for quantity discount information. Training manuals, CD-ROMs, and portions of this book are also available individually or can be tailored for specific needs.

ISBN: 1-59200-934-4
Library of Congress Catalog Card Number: 2005927428
Printed in Canada
05 06 07 08 09 PH 10 9 8 7 6 5 4 3 2

THOMSON

™

COURSE TECHNOLOGY

Professional ■ Technical ■ Reference

Thomson Course Technology PTR,
a division of Thomson Course Technology
25 Thomson Place
Boston, MA 02210
http://www.courseptr.com

Publisher and General Manager, Thomson Course Technology PTR:
Stacy L. Hiquet

Associate Director of Marketing:
Sarah O'Donnell

Manager of Editorial Services:
Heather Talbot

Marketing Manager:
Heather Hurley

Acquisitions Editor:
Mitzi Koontz

Senior Editor:
Mark Garvey

Marketing Coordinator:
Jordan Casey

Project Editor:
Sandy Doell

Editorial Services Coordinator:
Elizabeth Furbish

Interior Layout Tech:
Sue Honeywell

Cover Designer:
Mike Tanamachi

Indexer:
Kelly Talbot

Proofreader:
Sandi Wilson

To Marilyn Ginsburg Kindler, whose love of truth, creativity, and sensitive awareness have significantly influenced this book and its author.

Foreword

Times have changed—and as times have changed, leadership has changed. As a member of the Board of the Peter Drucker Foundation, I have had several opportunities to hear Peter share his views on the future. One of Peter's phrases I will never forget is: "The leader of the past knew how to *tell*. The leader of the future will know how to *ask*." In the new world of leadership, most of us manage people called "knowledge workers." In other words, they know more about what they are doing than we do! We can't just tell them what to do and how to do it. We have to ask, listen, and learn. As Herb notes, leadership will involve, "gaining commitment by inviting and focusing diverse insights that are not ego driven."

As part of a project for Accenture, we interviewed over 200 high potential leaders from 120 companies around the world. (This resulted in our book, *Global Leadership: The Next Generation.*) We asked these future leaders to describe the qualities of the ideal global leader of the future. One quality mentioned was *achieving personal mastery*. In simple terms, this means that future leaders will need to know themselves. They will need to understand their personal strengths, challenges, desires, and motivations. *Leadership Mastery* does a wonderful job of helping readers do just that. By responding to the self-assessment questions, reviewing your own profile, and working the case studies—you will not only learn about leadership, you will learn about yourself.

Another quality that was seen as critical for the global leader of the future is *building partnerships*. Herb provides many guidelines for building relationships that can not only be used with direct reports, they can be used with managers, peers, and partners outside the organization.

Finally, aside from being an executive educator, I am a Buddhist. My personal mission is to help people have a happy life.

I will never forget one day when I was teaching a leadership development session in an investment bank. One of the bank's executives gruffly asked, "Will any of this crap help us make money?"

I thought about his question and replied, "I think so. Your company thinks so. This will help you become a more effective leader of people. It will help you keep great people and build meaningful partnerships across the business."

For some reason, I went on to add: "But personally, I don't care if you make any more money. You are already worth millions of dollars. I would just like to help you and the people around you to have better lives. Do you have any objections to that?"

The banker looked at me, thought for a second and said, "Thank you. I really appreciate what you just said."

Will this book help your company become more productive? I think so. Will it help you become a better leader? Yes. Can this book help you to have a better life? Definitely!

As you read *Leadership Mastery*, don't critique the book. Critique yourself. Challenge yourself. Ask yourself the hard questions. Practice what you are learning to help yourself and the people around you to have better lives!

Marshall Goldsmith, Ph.D.

Dr. Marshall Goldsmith has recently been named by the American Management Association as one of 50 great thinkers and leaders who have influenced the field of management.

The Wall Street Journal named him as one of the top 10 executive educators; *Forbes*—as one of five most respected executive coaches; and *The Economist*—as one of the most credible thought leaders in the new era of business. He has been profiled in *The New Yorker* and *Harvard Business Review.*

Goldsmith is the co-editor or author of 19 books, including *The Leader of the Future* (a *BusinessWeek* bestseller), *Global Leadership: The Next Generation,* and *Coaching for Leadership.*

Acknowledgments

I want to acknowledge the leaders and aspiring leaders whose contributions to our skill-building workshops are distilled in this book. I want, also, to express my appreciation to Project Editor, Sandy Doell, for her discerning contributions as the book took its final form. Thank you to Marlene Caroselli for graciously permitting the inclusion of several ethical leadership tips from her book, *Leading Honorably* (Thomson Course Technology, A Crisp Fifty-Minute Book).

ABOUT THE AUTHOR

About **HERB KINDLER, Ph.D.:** This book reflects the views and distills the wisdom expressed during hundreds of leadership skill-building workshops—particularly those Herb conducted in recent years at the UCLA Technical Management Program and the UC Berkeley Project Leadership Program. Herb's leadership seminars are with such varied organizations as IBM, General Motors, U. S. Navy, Hughes Electronics, BBDO, Lockheed Martin, JVC, Boeing, Lawrence Livermore National Laboratory, TRW, Starbucks, AARP, Mattel Toys, Symantec, and companies in Milan, Mexico City, and Bangkok.

Dr. Kindler is an M.I.T. graduate in mechanical engineering, with a master's degree in public administration, and a doctorate in management from UCLA. He was a project manager, holding instrumentation patents, a chief engineer and CEO in industry before becoming full professor of management and organization behavior at Loyola Marymount University in Los Angeles. He currently conducts short courses at universities, corporations, and government organizations.

He has published seven books including, from Thomson Course Technology:

Managing Conflict, 3rd Edition

Risk Taking: A Guide for Decision Makers, Revised Edition

Clear and Creative Thinking

About the Contributing Author

Portions of this book were taken from *Leading Honorably* by MARLENE CAROSELLI, ED.D., published by Thomson Course Technology—A Crisp Fifty-Minute Book.

Dr. Caroselli is the author of 53 business books and is an international keynote speaker and corporate trainer for Fortune 100 companies, government agencies, educational institutions, and professional organizations.

She frequently contributes to many well-known publications (including Stephen Covey's *Excellence* publications and *National Business Employment Weekly*). Caroselli's first book, *The Language of Leadership,* was chosen as a main selection by Newbridge's Executive Development Book Club.

Her book, *Principled Persuasion,* was named a Director's Choice by Doubleday Book Club. Her latest book, *50 Activities for Promoting Ethics in the Organization,* has been co-released by HRD Press and the American Management Association.

Contents

Introduction

Turbulent, disruptive, unpredictable change, intense competition, complex global interdependence, and crumbling hierarchical structures demand rethinking leadership. For decades, leaders were expected to model organizationally correct behavior, determine what risks to take, and act as though they were firmly in control.

Now, peak performance requires more than traditional top-down planning-organizing-directing.

The emerging leadership paradigm involves gaining commitment by inviting and focusing diverse insights that are not ego driven. The new leader is a mentor-facilitator who orchestrates productive conversations that define direction, clarify values, fuel creativity, energize performance, and help people learn from their experience.

Leadership mastery requires flexible structures, collaborative processes, transformational creativity, and the passionate desire to make a difference. The new leader is introspective, shares insights, and helps people explore and express divergent perspectives. Leadership mastery paradoxically releases the traditional mandate for stability and control. Instead, leaders encourage open-ended inquiry and transformational change and are willing to expose their own vulnerability.

Both in organizational settings and in your personal life, leadership involves self-management skills, clear strategic thinking, and performance—topics examined via lively case studies, stimulating exercises, and in-depth discussion of challenges facing leaders in this era of turbulent times.

PART I

SELF

DEVELOPMENT

Knowing others is intelligence;
Knowing yourself is wisdom;
Acting on intelligence and
wisdom is leadership.

—Lao Tzu

Chapter 1

The
Introspective
Leader

"The wellspring of self-knowledge
is introspection—self-reflection
on our motives, prejudices,
actions, gifts, and graces."

—C. Michael Thompson

*I*n ancient China, a Taoist story tells of a young teacher who was directed to coach the monarch. Before embarking on this educational challenge, the teacher visited a wise man for counsel, explaining: "I am supposed to mentor the King, who is all-powerful, but arrogant and possessed of a murderous disposition. How shall I proceed?"

"The first thing you must do is not to improve the King, but yourself."

Leadership in turbulent times demands a fresh understanding and re-definition:

Leadership is a personal process anchored in mutual respect in which stakeholders choose the level at which they will contribute their energy and resources to advance shared goals and common values.

Leadership is not command and control power wielding. Power derives from hierarchical position, privileged information, charismatic oratory, the capacity to reward and punish, access to influential people, back scratching reciprocity, and leverage that limits action options available to others. Leadership evokes commitment; the exercise of power, at best, elicits compliance. Ultimate leadership mastery is its capacity to transform followers into leaders.

The starting point is *introspection*: gaining insight through self-witnessing.

Only when you see your programmed reactions can you challenge these patterned behaviors and the beliefs that support them.

For example, as a child, I was embarrassed by my undiagnosed dyslexia. It hindered my ability to read, memorize, and correctly pronounce unfamiliar words. To this day, despite largely over-coming what is a perceptual processing problem, I too often find myself still trying to prove I am "normal." Only by vigilantly retaining a level of consciousness—an *aware witness*—am I able to respond to current reality without the early baggage of hiding my deficiencies in counter-productive behavior.

A *Harvard Business Review* article, "How I Learned to Let My Workers Lead," by Ralph Stayer, described how he replaced his outworn beliefs and transformed followers to leaders.[1] Stayer owned a regional sausage processing company with average profits for his industry and a steady annual growth rate. Yet, he knew his firm was in a vulnerable competitive position from companies with national distribution. His insight (similar to the Taoist mentor to the Chinese King): "To fix the company, I would have to start by fixing myself."

Insights filtered through Stayer's "aware witness" as he exam-ined the following three assumptions he previously believed beyond question to be true.

- *Reasonable pay with periodic raises would assure a well-motivated workforce.* When he tested this belief with an anonymous employee survey, he learned that employees saw nothing for themselves at the company beyond a paycheck. They had little interest in cutting costs or improving quality.

- *Financially support only those activities that directly im-prove the bottom line.* On reflection, Stayer realized that people value learning—whether accounting, marketing, sky diving, or Italian cooking. He instituted a "learning allowance" for all employees who enrolled in educational programs irrespective of relevance to their work. Result: Employees felt recognized at a human level and reflected their appreciation through diligent performance and new respect for how the company valued its employees.

◆ *Decision-making should be a top down process.* His new conclusion: The best decision makers are those who have to implement decisions they make and have to live with the consequences. To improve quality control, for example, he shifted responsibility from management to teams of workers who tasted sausage every morning and discussed possible improvements. They also asked for cost data and customer reactions, resulting in both improved product and the design of a more useful and cost effective information processing system.

Over time, by developing a culture that questioned conventional wisdom and respected employees' capacity for creative problem solving, performance in the sausage factory steadily improved.

The following case, based on a true story, dramatizes the failure of Albert, an aspiring leader, to self-witness and update his early beliefs.

Case Study: The Summit

Raised in a fatherless home, Albert watched as his mother lifted the family from near poverty to a middle class suburban lifestyle by hard work and determination. Albert pitched in by delivering newspapers, mowing lawns, grooming dogs, and scouting for odd jobs. In high school, his photo punctuated the yearbook, displaying his ubiquitous presence in extracurricular club activities. At college, having won a full scholarship, he drove an airport shuttle for spending money. Within weeks of graduation, he married his high-school sweetheart, Carla, and accepted a management trainee position at Apex Electronics. His industry and dedication were rewarded with steady advancement and challenging assignments. He gained the reputation for being a demanding manager, as suggested by this interview.

> ALBERT: Maria, I like the good things I've been hearing about your performance, teamwork, and diligence. I'm looking for one more team member. Are you interested?
>
> MARIA: Definitely. Could you describe the work and what my role would be?
>
> ALBERT: We're reorganizing production around an all-new technology. Top management set a late September date for startup, but I intend to beat that date by at least five weeks. I want to start shipping product by mid-August. We can do it if every team member puts in 110 percent effort. I want my people to produce more, better, and faster—to show other departments what real producers can do.
>
> MARIA: You can count on me to give the team my best effort.
>
> ALBERT: I want to be clear about my management philosophy. I have no interest in excuses. For example, if making our August date means working nights and weekends, so be it. Whatever it takes, Maria; that's what I expect from my people.
>
> MARIA: I'm willing to give myself fully to the project during and occasionally beyond working hours. But, I have two small children at home and, after work, it's important to me to be with my family.
>
> ALBERT: Thanks for being candid. However, I want someone who can consistently meet my targets. Sorry.

Even though Albert maintained a relentless pace and long hours, he also found time for high visibility assignments such as serving as company coordinator for charity fund drives and contributing articles to the company newsletter.

As Apex Technology expanded, Albert's family moved to three different cities.

Albert made the moves cheerfully, apparently thriving on each fresh challenge. His wife Carla wondered if, without her knowledge, Albert had actually volunteered to transfer locations to better position himself for future promotions.

Carla accepted each move stoically as an implicit part of being an executive's wife. Uncharacteristically, she openly opposed the fourth move, which Albert planned to accept. One evening, in Albert's study, Carla made her case.

CARLA: Hon, let's talk about the question of moving. I realize it's a promotion for you. But, really, the children deserve better than another disruption at school and another round of making new friends.

ALBERT: I haven't discussed this with you, but this move to corporate headquarters is more than a promotion—it caps my career. It's what I've been aiming at all these years. I'll be part of the executive team, reporting to the vice president, Lou. And, I'll be in line for his job when he retires in two years.

CARLA: Bud has five months to finish his high school junior year. He'll get into a good college if we don't pull him out now. Albert, we already have enough money. It doesn't make sense to move again.

ALBERT: Carla, this is what I've worked hard to achieve. I'm not going to let it slip through my fingers. Arrange for Bud to stay with the O'Connors until he finishes the term. I'm going to tell Lou tomorrow that I'll start immediately.

CARLA: Please, wait a week. Give yourself time so you can be sure you're thinking clearly.

ALBERT: Carla, the matter is settled. Call our realtor in the morning and let's get going.

While Carla arranged for selling their home, and preparing the children for their next move, Albert started his new job. He had six managers reporting to him, including one who failed to meet his standards—José. Albert sent him a written warning. José was furious as he entered Albert's office saying: "I've worked here for 20 years and nobody, but nobody, ever had a problem with my performance. Who do you think you are to come here with zero experience in this operation and to start learning by criticizing. I want an apology and I want your memo out of my personnel file now."

Albert wasn't accustomed to having his authority challenged. He replied in an angry tone: "José, clean up your act or you're on your way out!"

José went straight to Lou's office. Thirty minutes later, Albert was shocked when his boss phoned to say: "Rescind the memo you sent José, take time to review the situation, and let's meet." Albert's initiation included other disagreements. Sometimes his views prevailed; other times he had no choice but to give in.

During his second month at headquarters, Lou gave him a totally new assignment. "I'm taking you out of operations. I want you to focus on strategic planning."

About six weeks into his new planning function, Albert experienced extreme physical discomfort, nausea, diarrhea, and insomnia. Having always had robust health, he was alarmed and confided in Lou: "I'm worried. I can't concentrate on my work, and I'm irritable much of the time."

"Al, I want you to see a doctor. And, I notice you are still holding on to operational tasks I asked you to delegate. Your job is to sit back and dream creatively about the company's future. I want you to take time away from the office to develop long-term strategy. And, let me know what the doctor has to say."

Two weeks later, Albert's wife phoned Lou: "The doctor said there's nothing physically wrong. He prescribed a long vacation and rest."

Lou urged Albert to take the doctor's advice. Three weeks into his Hawaiian vacation, Albert's stomach cramps got so bad, he and Carla flew home where he was hospitalized for more tests. When nothing definitive showed up, the doctor again suggested "lots of rest, take life easy, slow down at work."

Instead of bouncing back, Albert became deeply depressed. Within a month he committed suicide.

Case Study Questions and Answers

Please record your response to the following questions:

What were the core problems in Albert's career and life?

_____

_____

_____

_____

_____

How might he have dealt with them in ways that were likely to be satisfying and effective?

_____

_____

_____

_____

_____

If you had been Albert's supervisor at the time when he interviewed Maria (assume Maria complained to you about Albert's "anti-family" job requirements), how would you have coached Albert?

_____

_____

_____

_____

_____

Case Study Discussion

Albert became a prisoner of his own unexamined beliefs. What he saw as a child was that hard work and relentless effort yielded a "desirable" lifestyle. But, instead of reviewing and reassessing his own personal vision over time, he steered a course through life set on automatic pilot. His single-minded focus was to reach the top irrespective of human cost. For example, Albert didn't attempt to develop creative possibilities when Maria said she was concerned about spending enough time with her children. He didn't even think about exposing his company to a potential discrimination lawsuit. Albert didn't discuss with his wife the impact on his own family if he moved them to another city. He was also unilateral in his approach to a new direct report, José, about perceived unsatisfactory performance. In other words, missing from Albert's leadership toolkit was the art of *collaboration*.

With Albert's mind rigidly set on corporate advancement, he didn't look inward to understand that leadership is a multidimensional process that includes concern for the wellbeing of others while also focusing on creativity, performance, and learning.

Because of Albert's activity-oriented rush to the top, he didn't take time to think strategically. Even at a tactical level, Albert erred by putting all his "eggs" in one basket—his career basket. When the eggs broke, he was devastated, feeling crushed with no contingency plan. Albert's do-or-die philosophy was literally descriptive of his worldview, foreshadowing his stress-attacks and ultimate suicide.

Because of his obsessive goal orientation, Albert's life satisfaction lay in the future, not in the present. He aimed at a destination and missed the journey. He sacrificed living now on the altar of future gratification. Albert could have benefited from the philosophy of Zorba, the fictional character in Kazantzakis's *Zorba The Greek*, who said:

"What's happening today, this minute,
that's what I care about. I say:

'What are you doing at this moment, Zorba?'

'I'm sleeping.'

'Well, sleep well.'

'What are you doing at this moment, Zorba?'

'I'm working.'

'Well, work well.'

'What are you doing at this moment, Zorba?'

'I'm kissing a woman.'

'Well, kiss her well.
And forget all the rest
while you are doing it;
there's nothing else on earth,
only you and her!
Get on with it.'" [2]

The case study also suggests a basic existential issue. Albert's life seems rooted in the stress-evoking belief that his worthiness is a variable. Every day he must prove his value; he must achieve something. On the other hand, if Albert believed that he is inherently worthy, that "God doesn't make junk,"[3] he could go through life more relaxed, more willing to flow, less reluctant to surrender control.

In summary, Albert—like many of us—could have realized a more satisfying and productive life through a balanced lifestyle—balance between action and reflection, between doing and being. Through spiritual inquiry and introspection, Albert could have appreciated that being worthy is everyone's birthright, not a variable that endlessly drains energy. Although leaders are guided by intention and vision, they can only be effective and satisfied in the present, not in the fantasy of some vague, future, hoped for reality.

Exercise in Introspection

Identify a *pattern* in your life that helps you better understand how you deal with difficult situations or interpersonal friction.

_____

_____

_____

Who had an important, enduring influence on your life? What was one impact this person had?

_____

_____

_____

Have you made a life altering decision that you now regret? If you could retrace your steps, what would you do differently?

_____

_____

_____

What one experience do you want to have, or what one contribution do you want to make before you die?

_____

_____

_____

What was a significant life ending? Consider relationships, career, relocation, a death, loss of innocence. What impact did it have? What impact does it still have?

_____

_____

_____

Leading Honorably Tip: Define Irreducible Essences

On his deathbed, U.S. Senator Hubert Humphrey spoke about the "irreducible essence." In other words, when all else is stripped away, what is it that you stand for? For Humphrey, it was love of country.

What lies at your core? What defines you as a man or woman? As a leader? To lead honorably is to know what matters most. That essence should come through loud and clear to your followers. They must know what you stand for before they can choose to make your cause their own.

By articulating a values statement, you are simultaneously making a pledge to lead honorably. Thus, you emerge a winner. So, too, will your followers—for they are committing to a cause that may not have success guaranteed but will have, at least, an ethical path to follow.

It has been said that if you doubt the power of a single individual to effect positive change, then you have never been in bed with a mosquito! On a more serious note, consider that Nobel Peace Prize winner Lech Walesa invited nine others to meet with him on the need for reform in the Polish government. A month later, that number had grown to 95 million.

In the words of cultural anthropologist Margaret Mead, "Never doubt that a small group of thoughtful, committed citizens can change the world; indeed, it is the only thing that ever has."

Define Your Essence

◆ What are your essential values?

_____

_____

_____

_____

◆ If you were to leave your organization within the next year, what legacy would you like to leave behind?

_____

_____

_____

_____

◆ What leadership project could you take on to share those values and realize that legacy?

_____

_____

_____

_____

◆ Write the name of a person or group that could be viewed as a winner from learning what you have articulated as your irreducible essence.

_____

_____

_____

_____

◆ Describe, as specifically as you can, how this person or group would benefit from this knowledge.

_____

_____

_____

_____

CHAPTER 2
WHERE IS THE TRUTH?

**Truth is rarely pure
and never simple.**

—Oscar Wilde

*J*ack Welsh, General Electric's former CEO, said: "No one at GE loses a job because of an unprofitable quarter, a bad year, or a mistake. People are given second chances. There's only one performance failure where there is no second chance. That's a clear violation of integrity." [1]

Unvarnished truth is the gold standard of leadership. If managers can't be trusted to tell the truth—without spin, sugar coating, rationalization, exaggeration, or cover-up—why would you trust them with a truth that leaves you vulnerable?

At one point in my career, I was technical director reporting to CEO "John." On the surface we made a good team with my background in engineering and his in marketing. But, John put more energy into ingratiating himself with our board of directors than supporting employees. Despite his focus on "sucking up" to board members, the organization prospered. At one point, I suggested to John that we develop a retirement plan for the staff. His response: "Great idea." Later, when I asked, he told me the board turned down the proposal as too costly. Still later, I learned that he sold the board on a lucrative retirement deal exclusively for himself and never proposed anything for other employees. From the moment I discovered John's lie until he retired two years later, I felt intense distrust and the need to be ever-vigilant with him. John had violated the twin foundation on which trust is built—truth telling and fair dealing.

Model: Trust and Leader Influence

People in leadership positions enhance their influence to the degree that they are seen as trustworthy. They earn this perception by impeccably keeping their word and by honest disclosure without self-serving spin. The relationship between trust and leader influence is shown in this model.

		Level of Trust in Leader	
		LOW	HIGH
Leader Influence	Leader Gives Positive Feedback	Feedback Discounted as Manipulative	Feedback Accepted as Earned Recognition
	Leader Gives Negative Feedback	Feedback Rejected as a Ploy to Shift Blame	Feedback Accepted as Coaching or Mentoring

Nowhere has lying been more dramatically punished than in the office of the United States President. After the public learned that he lied about authorizing a break-in at the Democratic Party's Watergate headquarters, Richard Nixon was forced to resign. This loss of public trust not only ended his political career, it tarnished even his positive accomplishments, such as his ground-breaking trip to Communist China, gaining Soviet agreement to limit nuclear arms, and his creation of the Environmental Protection Agency. Similarly, Bill Clinton lost his power to lead after he lied to the public about his affair with Monica Lewinsky.

Truth is distorted when a good face is put on some harsh reality. I recall a woman who wanted friends to see her promiscuous daughter in a favorable light. The language she used to hide the truth was: "My daughter had an *unfortunate overlap* between Husband #1 and Husband #2."

Truth is rarely black or white. It depends on context. Put yourself in this situation:

In an office setting, your manager asks her perfunctory morning question: "How are you today?" She probably doesn't want to know that your kids were late for school, the washing machine overflowed on new carpeting, and at breakfast your spouse confessed to an affair with your best friend.

If you reply, "I'm fine," rather than "I'm a basket case," are you lying? Or, are you being truthful to your understanding of your boss's implicit question: "Can you handle what needs to be done today?"

Truth can be hidden non-verbally. When my father wanted a reduced doctor's bill, he wore stained work clothes to office visits—hiding the truth that while his stains reflected honest labor, he owned a reasonably successful plumbing and heating business.

Distorting the truth—and, by truth, I don't mean tactless honesty—imposes a significant cost. You reduce the opportunity to learn from your experience. For example, in my father's desire to pay his doctor less than the going rate, he side-stepped asking himself such introspective "learning" questions as: "Do I believe the physician is trying to take advantage of me? Am I envious that the doctor doesn't have to clean stopped up sewers and overflowing toilets?" My father was an immigrant who arrived in the United States at sixteen barely able to speak English. Did he resent not having the education that might have lifted him to the social and financial status of a physician?

Truth is also distorted when words are sanitized, such as "de-hiring" "reducing head count," or "right-sizing." The reality of flesh-and-blood people losing their jobs, livelihood, and even their homes is trivialized. Similarly, the horror of war, with its killing and maiming of innocent civilians, is obscured in terms like "surgical strikes," "smart bombs," and "collateral damage."

Truth can be concealed in language itself. When I was a consultant for a West Coast ad agency, a common complaint of several staff people was: "The president doesn't give me straight feedback on new ideas. Instead his pat response: *"I don't disagree with you."*

Does his double negative mean:

I do agree with you?

I agree to some limited extent?

I don't agree, but I want you to believe I agree?

I agree, but I don't think your idea is feasible or important?

Family secrets also side-step truth. When I was seven, my parents hid the fact from me that my grandmother died. On learning the truth from a cousin, my reaction was confusion and fear about the meaning of death.

Truth is often deflected by denial. Despite the speech defect that haunted my childhood, the topic was never discussed by my parents who didn't want to confront this troubling reality. Once, without explanation, my mother did take me to a Manhattan speech clinic. I had instant revulsion to patients who made frightening guttural sounds. After my second visit, still hidden from the fresh air of open discussion, my speech therapy was summarily dropped.

Deflecting unpleasant truths inhibits authentic human connection. When I was eight, an older boy with gross physical deformities—beyond what upset me at the speech clinic—moved into our neighborhood. He limped grotesquely, scraping one foot behind him along the pavement, while his tortured body lurched as he made slow progress. I was scared to go near him. The truth of his affliction was never acknowledged by my family. In the absence of confronting this reality, I didn't understand that what this handicapped person desperately needed was someone to befriend him, someone with whom he could connect—even with a nod, smile, or "good morning."

Years later, my first personal understanding of the power of truth came during a conversation with a woman. One evening, I told her of the boy whose deformities were so frightening to me. In turn, Ruth's story was of a young man in her neighborhood who walked on a wooden leg. Rather than being hesitant to engage him, she was intrigued. During their talks, Ruth asked him if he unscrewed his leg when he went to bed. And, did he oil it? I was astounded to learn that some people actually spoke truthfully about potentially painful and embarrassing topics. They communicated what was real for them. I learned, if I want to connect meaningfully with another human being (and—more importantly—with myself), the pathway is impeccable truth.

Not only is truth buried by not discussing sensitive topics, it is violated in broken promises. When adult children borrow from their parents, for example, they often develop "discretionary amnesia"—so common, at least in Western cultures, that one wag advises women: "Never loan money to anyone to whom you have given birth."

Intentional deceit is sometimes appropriate. Imagine yourself hiding a Jewish child from the Gestapo in France during World War II. You open your front door to two Nazi soldiers.

**"Do you have any children
hidden in your home?
Tell us the truth and no harm
will come to you."**

Would you tell the truth?

During my second year at college I experienced a sharp pain in my side. Fellow students rushed me to a surgeon's office. When I almost collapsed in agonizing pain, the doctor examined me, cancelled his office hours, and personally drove me to a nearby hospital. During the ride, he told me immediate surgery was vital but, because I was a minor, he needed my parents' permission to operate. He said every minute counted because my appendix appeared ready to burst. I was checked in, rolled outside the operating room, and handed a telephone. I heard the doctor's voice ask me (he called from a nearby phone making believe he was speaking with my parent) for permission to operate on "my son." I trusted this doctor and went along with the lie, "granting permission."

In both examples, the Gestapo and the surgeon, the intent in lying was neither for personal gain nor to avoid embarrassment. The critical value—human life—was more compelling than truth.

The question my executive coach wife often asks herself, me, and her clients:

"Where is the truth?"
Or, she opens to truth through
a back door by asking:
"How am I deceiving myself?"

Truthfulness is tested when it collides with other values. For example, at work, you may learn of a one-time air pollution accident not reported by your staff to government authorities to shield your company from fines. You experience the conflict between exposing the truth and rationalizing the incident as a one-time aberration.

Leadership starts within—being honest with yourself to find your own truth. On the following page is an exercise to help you steer your life toward what really matters to you by making the truth of your personal vision explicit.

The Truth About Your Personal Vision

When you are not sleeping or eating what percent of your time do you currently spend with:		When you are not sleeping or eating what percent of your time do you want to spend with:
_____	Your job and commuting	_____
_____	Romance and intimacy	_____
_____	Professional development	_____
_____	Recreation, play, exercise	_____
_____	Personal finance, budgeting	_____
_____	Entertainment, TV, Internet	_____
_____	Family conversation	_____
_____	Spiritual pursuits	_____
_____	Time with friends	_____
_____	Vacation, travel, in nature	_____
_____	Personal growth	_____
_____	Service	_____
_____	Creative expression	_____
_____	Rest, relaxation, reading	_____
_____	Shopping	_____
_____	Maintenance, grooming	_____
_____	Other:	_____
100%		100%

The clarity you gain from this exercise clears space for a more positive, productive, and passionate life to manifest. But don't defer this self-searching examination. In his poem, *The Love Song of J. Alfred Prufrock*, T. S. Eliot captures the wistful sadness of waiting too long.[2]

I grow old... I grow old...
I shall wear the bottoms
of my trousers rolled
Shall I part my hair behind?
Do I dare to eat a peach?
I shall wear white flannel trousers,
and walk upon the beach.

Space for leadership is opened when, as the Bible suggests, "The truth shall set you free."

Leading Honorably Tip: Earn Trust

Sixteen hundred years ago, St. Augustine wrote, "When regard for trust has been broken down or even slightly weakened, all things will remain doubtful." However unintentional the weakening may be, when integrity is compromised, little is left. If you are sending messages that—deliberately or inadvertently—are eroding trust, your efforts may become suspect and your best intentions may be doubted.

Leading honorably means earning trust, yes. But it also means continuing to regard that trust as a precious entity, one that must be protected throughout the life of the relationship between leader and followers.

Assess Your Earned Trust

♦ Are you certain you have the trust of your followers?

_____

♦ If yes, then how do you know you have that trust?

_____

_____

_____

_____

♦ If no, then take the following actions:
  ♦ Meet with your followers—one-on-one if they do not know you well or if something has happened to lessen their faith in you.
  ♦ Talk to your followers about your track record, which should reflect the reasons that others have trusted you.
  ♦ Ask your followers what you can do to earn their trust.

CHAPTER 3
HOW YOU KNOW

God, guard me against
thoughts men think
in the mind alone;
He who sings a lasting song
also thinks in the marrow bone

—William Butler Yeats

*L*eaders need clarity accessible via the two fundamental ways of understanding reality: *linear reasoning* and *inner knowing.* Gaining synergy between these dual pathways enables leaders to focus attention and unleash energy.

Linear Reasoning

Most business thinking is driven by *analytical reasoning*—cutting through subjective speculation to get at the hard facts. This orientation is reinforced by the desire of leaders to be seen as no-nonsense decision-makers who examine objective evidence and make judgments based on impersonal logic.

Linear reasoning uses cause-and-effect analysis embedded in Western cultures since the dawn of the Age of Reason. To "reasonable" people, numbers are what "count." As children, we begin to see the impact of numbers on our lives—admission into good schools depends on test scores. Public policy is built on demographic numbers, gross domestic product, and per capita income. Leisure is punctuated with sports statistics, gross box office receipts for new movies, and the fluctuation of stock market indices.

Reasoning infers thoughts from prior thoughts. It assesses idea validity and utility. People whose primary mode of understanding is cognitive depend on, suggests Stanford University's Harold Leavitt, "the language of numbers, dividing problems into components, seeking operational decision rules, and searching for convergence—that is, *an* answer." Leavitt says managers, in particular, "test logic by trying to poke holes in reasoning, look for internal inconsistencies, the inability to replicate experiments, and other methodological weaknesses."[1]

Dispassionate reasoning is inescapably essential in almost every facet of our complex, technological lives. Reasoning enables you to lose pounds by counting calories, record a TV program, develop a cost-benefit analysis, take the right vitamins, and understand why there are funny noises under the hood of your car.

In her book *The Artist's Way*, Julia Cameron says "the 'logic brain' thinks in neat, linear fashion perceiving the world according to known categories. To the logic brain, a horse is a certain combination of parts that make up the animal."[2]

Cameron may have borrowed her example of a horse from Charles Dickens, who, in *Hard Times*, has pretentious, fact-obsessed headmaster Gradgrind instructing his class by asking a student:

"Blitzer, your definition of a horse."

**"Quadruped. Graminivorous.
Forty teeth, namely twenty-four grinders,
four eye teeth and twelve incisors.
Sheds coat in the spring; in marshy countries,
sheds hoofs too. Hoofs hard but requiring
to be shod with iron.
Age known by marks in mouth."**

**"Now," said Mr. Gradgrind to his class,
"you know what a horse is."**

People who use reasoned knowing alone miss a lot of life's rich texture. Other areas of potential weakness—when reasoned knowing is the dominant mode by which you know what you know—are one's vulnerability to *stereotypical bias, rationalization, unfounded assumptions,* and *false data* (such as "spin" and "hype").

Suppose you are told that following a grueling automobile race, a young person, Tom, wants to congratulate the winner. When stopped by security guards, he claims to be the winning driver's son. Frustrating Tom, however, is the fact that the driver emphatically denies being his father. How could Tom and the winning driver both be telling the truth?

Because of the tendency to *stereotype* race-car drivers as macho and masculine, it is easy to miss the conclusion that the driver is Tom's *mother.*

Another common human trait is *rationalization*—the desire to appear reasonable to others and to oneself. Faced with a decision that went awry, we tend to justify, defend and explain away our misjudgment. Albert Camus, reflecting on this tendency to *rationalize* (a term coined by Freud), concluded that people are creatures who spend their lives attempting to convince themselves they are not absurd.

Unwarranted assumptions can also upset the reasoning process. For example, my wife and I tried to get an estimate from a Mexican-American house painter. We decided, because Marilyn was more adept than I at languages, she should make the phone call. The painter's wife answered the phone, didn't speak a word of English, and quickly gave the phone to her husband. Because Marilyn is fluent in Italian, we assumed this would be the linguistic bridge. After much communication confusion and mutual frustration, the painter politely asked:

"Excuse me please, anyone in your house speak English?"

Perhaps the most concerning aspect of cold reasoning, when used alone, is its inability to spark passion, spur commitment, inspire creativity, or energize performance. It needs to be balanced with inner knowing.

Inner Knowing

Using its innate wisdom, the body circulates blood, digests food, and fights infection. To some degree, you can tap the amazing gift of inner knowing by paying attention to visceral and intuitive cues, and what "feels right." Relax your body and clear your mind. Meditation helps—whether counting out-breaths, repeating a phrase, or reciting a prayer. Alan Watts observed:

> **"Meditation is the art of suspending thinking for a time, somewhat as a courteous audience will stop talking when a concert is about to begin."**[3]

"Ronald Reagan reached conclusions," reported *The Economist* when the ex-president died, "not by spending 18 hours a day rationally assembling facts and figures. He knew that reason alone, essential though it is, is only half the business of reaching momentous decisions. Also needed are instincts and feelings."[4]

Yale historian Carlos Eire, in receiving the 2003 National Book Award, said:

> **"I was guided by images rather than linear reasoning. I would have an image of some event and then constructed an entire chapter around that image.
> I didn't map the book out.
> I didn't outline it.
> I didn't reason it through."**[5]

Author Julia Cameron defines "artist's brain" as "associative and free-wheeling, our inventor, connecting with a source of inner wisdom."

Two pathways to inner knowing are *intuition* and *dream-work*.

Intuition

The dictionary definition of intuition: "knowing obtained without recourse to inference, analysis, or logic." Intuition is a direct, holistic inner experience that bypasses the cognitive part of the brain—probably a self-protective mechanism. When a primitive caveman heard a twig snap, he needed to act instantly against what might be a dangerous intruder.

Should you want to experiment (mischievously) with a golfing friend, you can test the power of intuitive knowing. Before she tees off, ask: "When you raise your club above your head poised to swing into the ball, *do you breathe in or out?*" This tactic is unlikely to be appreciated because it disrupts a smooth stroke by introducing conscious awareness where *inner knowing* is the best executive for the job.

Harnessing the power of intuition requires capturing those unexpected insights that dart into your consciousness hinting at a direction for you to take. When, as CEO, I hired an operations manager,

I ignored my hunch that the candidate lacked leadership. My rational mind said: "Herb, you have solid factual evidence—this guy was an army major." I ran right through my intuitive warning signals. My gut feeling turned out to be the more accurate performance predictor. He did poorly until I transferred him to a technical staff position.

Dream-Work

By dream-work, I mean the process of recording, decoding, and understanding dream messages. The expression, "Let's sleep on it," reflects the common belief that dreams tap inner wisdom. The challenge is to understand in what direction a dream is pointing you.

In sleep laboratories, research confirms that, except when sedated, all human beings dream—whether or not they recall their dreams.[6] The wonder is why an activity that involves the entire human race isn't better understood.

Getting practical help with everyday problems is a realistic expectation of dream-work. When Robert Louis Stevenson was financially distressed, he asked his "dream brownies" for a marketable plot. "They" came through with the story of man's double nature that Stevenson developed into his psychological thriller: *The Strange Case of Dr. Jekyll and Mr. Hyde.* [7]

Similarly, Elias Howe needed practical help. He was stymied in perfecting his sewing machine invention and getting it to market ahead of competitors. In one of his dreams, he conjured up the bizarre scene of hungry cannibals capturing and plunging him into boiling water. Howe's attempts to escape becoming their dinner were foiled as the determined natives poked him back into the bubbling cauldron with spears—each oddly fashioned with a hole near the tip. When Howe awoke, dripping in sweat, he realized the thread transport needle of his sewing machine needed its hole pierced not at the blunt end—where it was located during centuries of hand sewing—but at the sharp end. Voilà, the sewing machine needle was born. Dreams may embrace multiple meanings. Howe, for example, also was in "hot water" with impatient investors.[8]

Beyond offering practical clues, psychologist Fritz Perls believed that dreams reflected disowned aspects of one's true nature. He built on Freud's hypothesis that adverse childhood experiences, too difficult to handle at an early age, are stored in the unconscious where they can be released to conscious awareness via dreams as stimuli for personal integration.[9]

Recurring dreams may be metaphors for real-life situations signaling unresolved conflict. They may be the medium through which your inner knowing tries to communicate with your aware consciousness.

Consider the following process for receiving dream communications.

- Keep a pencil and pad, or recording device, near your bed.
- When you awake, remain in a reverie state—part-awake, part-asleep—until a dream or dream fragment surfaces for you to record.
- Give yourself time to re-experience the dream and give it a *title* that captures its theme.
- Write your dream's *qualities* (vivifying, heavy, intimidating).
- List your dream's *elements* (people, places, things).
- Reflection: Go back into your dream to explore what personal meaning it may hold for you. If the dream suggests an *action* or *direction* for you to take, consider it. Vaughan writes: "Everything in a dream takes its meaning from the context of one's life, and it is always the dreamer who is the best intuitive interpreter of his or her dream."[10]

To illustrate this process, here's a dream fragment I recorded—written in the first person, present tense.

Dream: I am playing with and feeding five frisky dachshunds. I love these dogs.

Title: Nurturing

Qualities: Love, Connection, Play, Feeding

Elements: Me, Dachshunds, Food

Reflection: What comes into my awareness is the time I brought home a dachshund puppy who was raised with our babies. The puppy, named Servo, was treated as a full-fledged family member. Our babies nibbled on her floppy ears, sometimes—when we weren't looking—they shared her dog food, and once my son Alex coated her fur from head to tail with a white greasy cream intended to soothe his diaper rash. Three years later, Servo had six of her own puppies. Unfortunately, the veterinarian said her milk couldn't sustain them. I left work when I learned that Servo would not let my wife nor children near her—she never before had bared her teeth nor growled menacingly. On my way home I bought a doll's baby bottle to feed milk to the puppies. When I looked into Servo's sad brown eyes, I melted and hugged her. She trusted me. I spent the entire night, lying on the cold Pittsburgh basement floor next to her and an electric heater, feeding each tiny puppy through the night. All but one survived.

The *direction* this dream pointed me toward is to appreciate more deeply my joy when I am nurturing and mentoring others.

The following inventory helps you see your preferences in processing information (such as use of logical reasoning and intuitive synthesis) when decision-making and problem-solving.

"How-U-Know" Profile

This self-scoring profile reflects how you make sense of your reality. Following are pairs of statements that describe alternative behaviors. For each pair of statements, allocate *exactly 3 points* between the alternatives to show how frequently *you behave as described—not what you regard as ideal behavior.* Use only whole numbers—no fractions—based on this scoring key:

3 = *very often*	1 = *occasionally*
2 = *moderately often*	0 = *rarely or never*

There are no right or wrong answers.

1A.   ❑   I choose friends with whom I share intellectual interests.

1B.   ❑   I choose friends with whom I feel an empathic connection.

2A.   ❑   I primarily rely on logic when making career decisions.

2B.   ❑   I primarily rely on my instincts when making career decisions.

3A.   ❑   I consider qualitative factors (like my gut feelings) before investing.

3B.   ❑   I weigh quantitative factors (like market trends) before investing.

4A.   ❑   When my analysis and intuition are in conflict, I give precedence to my intuitive insights.

4B.   ❑   When my analysis and intuition are in conflict, I give precedence to my analytical reasoning.

5A.   ❑   I am attracted to people who are intellectually stimulating.

5B.   ❑   I am attracted to people who are emotionally expressive.

6A.   ❑   The most important factor in making a radical life change is feeling it is right for me.

6B.   ❑   The most important factor in making a radical life change is knowing that the change is based on objective, verifiable facts.

7A.   ❑   When making important decisions, I pay attention to such signals as a "knowing in my bones," or other physical sensations.

7B. ❑   When making important decisions, I pay attention to data relevant to my analysis.

8A. ❑   I am cautious about accepting conclusions of others when their reasoning is not supported by objective evidence.

8B. ❑   I am cautious about accepting conclusions of others when they have not been personally or emotionally involved.

9A. ❑   I am inclined to accept a person's proposal when I believe he or she has grasped the whole picture.

9B. ❑   I am inclined to accept a person's proposal when I believe he or she has based the proposal on verifiable facts.

10A. ❑   When an unforeseen event occurs, I systematically plan an appropriate response.

10B. ❑   When an unforeseen event occurs, I spontaneously improvise as a means to develop an appropriate response.

11A. ❑   To persuade others to appreciate my view, I look for a metaphor that captures the crucial points I want to make.

11B. ❑   To persuade others to appreciate my view, I walk them through my reasoning process.

12A. ❑   When I am not clear about what course of action to take, I prefer an incremental, step-by-step approach.

12B. ❑   When I am not clear about what course of action to take, I prefer to immerse myself in the issue and wait until I get an "aha" insight.

13A. ❑   Before starting a project, I prefer to collect data on which to base my approach.

13B.   ❑   Before starting a project, I prefer to visualize my desired outcome as a roadmap on which to base my approach.

Allocate a total of 3 points between each of the two words or phrases below using this scoring key:

3 = *very strong influence on how I behave*   2 = *strong influence on how I behave*

1 = *moderate influence on how I behave*   0 = *little or no influence on how I behave*

14A. ❑ Instinct		**23A.** ❑ Objectivity
14B. ❑ Intellect		**23B.** ❑ Subjectivity
15A. ❑ Scripted		**24A.** ❑ Improvise
15B. ❑ Extemporaneous		**24B.** ❑ Plan
16A. ❑ Experiment		**25A.** ❑ Felt Sense
16B. ❑ Experience		**25B.** ❑ Reason
17A. ❑ Synthesize		**26A.** ❑ Orderly
17B. ❑ Analyze		**26B.** ❑ Spontaneous
18A. ❑ Feelings		**27A.** ❑ Visualize
18B. ❑ Facts		**27B.** ❑ Verify
19A. ❑ Infer		**28A.** ❑ Data
19B. ❑ Imagine		**28B.** ❑ Hunch
20A. ❑ Possibility		**29A.** ❑ Tune In
20B. ❑ Evidence		**29B.** ❑ Figure Out
21A. ❑ Reflection		**30A.** ❑ Systematic
21B. ❑ Action		**30B.** ❑ Leap
22A. ❑ Conceptual		
22B. ❑ Emotional		

Transfer numbers you inserted on the previous pages to the designated boxes below. Add each of the four columns. The total sum of all four columns must equal 90. Note that As and Bs are reversed for some questions.

1B. ❏	1A. ❏	16B. ❏	16A. ❏
2A. ❏	2B. ❏	17B. ❏	17A. ❏
3B. ❏	3A. ❏	18A. ❏	18B. ❏
4A. ❏	4B. ❏	19B. ❏	19A. ❏
5B. ❏	5A. ❏	20A. ❏	20B. ❏
6B. ❏	6A. ❏	21A. ❏	21B. ❏
7B. ❏	7A. ❏	22A. ❏	22B. ❏
8A. ❏	8B. ❏	23B. ❏	23A. ❏
9B. ❏	9A. ❏	24B. ❏	24A. ❏
10A. ❏	10B. ❏	25A. ❏	25B. ❏
11B. ❏	11A. ❏	26B. ❏	26A. ❏
12A. ❏	12B. ❏	27A. ❏	27B. ❏
13A. ❏	13B. ❏	28B. ❏	28A. ❏
14B. ❏	14A. ❏	29A. ❏	29B. ❏
15A. ❏	15B. ❏	30B. ❏	30A. ❏

Col. 1 _____ Col. 2 _____ Col. 3 _____ Col. 4 _____

SCORING:

Column 1 + Column 3 = ____ Your Linear Reasoning Score

Column 2 + Column 4 = ____ Your Inner Knowing Score

SCORING INTERPRETATION

Preference for Linear Reasoning

If your Linear Reasoning score is 54 or higher, your *definite preference* is to problem-solve and reach decisions based on inferential-logical reasoning.

If your Linear Reasoning score is between 48 and 53, your *moderate preference* is for inferential-logical reasoning.

Preference for Inner Knowing

If your Inner Knowing score is 54 or higher, your *definite preference* is to problem-solve and reach decisions based on visceral-intuitive feelings.

If your Inner Knowing score is between 48 and 53, your *moderate preference* is for visceral-intuitive feelings.

Preference Neutral

If your Linear Reasoning and Inner Knowing scores are both less than 48, you don't have a strong reasoned or inner knowing preference and do have the *flexibility* to choose between the two based on each specific situation.

The figure to the right illustrates how the reasoned and inner modes of knowing interact synergistically to facilitate problem-solving and decision-making.

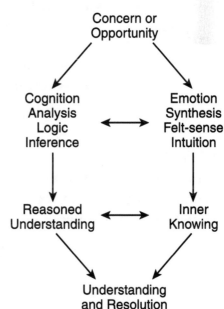

Gaining Synergy

The How-U-Know Profile aims at heightening your awareness of the two complementary ways you understand and appreciate your reality. The scoring suggests where to focus attention to gain synergy by more fully developing your less-preferred style of knowing.

Master cellist Pablo Casals wanted a student soloist to gain synergy. He chided: "You have played the notes; now also play the music." Translating this injunction to organizational environments: "You have grasped the situation with your rational mind; now blend logic with your intuitive sense."

If your strong preference is for linear reasoning, screenwriting coach Robert McKee, cautions:

**"Most executives attempt
to persuade people by
using an intellectual process,
building a case with a
PowerPoint slide presentation,
giving statistics and facts
and quotes from authorities.
That's not good enough,
because people are not inspired
to act by reason alone."**[11]

On the other hand, a strong preference for inner knowing may lead to decisions made prematurely in the sway of passion. Emotion unbridled from reason can lead to manipulation. Neurologist Donald Calne writes:

> "The capacity to manipulate
> an emotion is illustrated
> by the anti-Semitism
> of the Third Reich.
> By skillfully orchestrating
> a propaganda campaign,
> it proved possible
> to promulgate a hodgepodge
> of truths, half-truths,
> and untruths so that
> Jews became a national scapegoat."[12]

Gaining balance in how you know is not easy. As Harvard's Michael McCaskey observed: "The difficult trick is to combine in oneself such opposites as playfulness and rigorous discipline, intuition, and analytical thinking." [13]

Google's CEO Eric Schmidt attributes the spectacular rise of his company to the balance between "order, rigor, and discipline on one hand, and chaotic, irreverent innovation on the other."[14]

After you have a visceral feeling for an issue and its potential resolution, good sense suggests checking it out by sifting evidence, analyzing consequences, and evaluating alternatives. A striking example of how an intuitive flash can be validated through meticulous reasoning and diligent follow-up is a case involving New York City detective Andy Rosenzweig. He recalled:

"I was driving up Third Avenue
when I passed the corner
where a murdered man had
owned a bar and grill.
Suddenly, I experienced
a jolt of memory
and felt in my bones that
the murderer was still alive—
even though the case was closed
27 years before."

The crime had been witnessed
by the murdered man's girlfriend,
yet, despite knowing the killer's
identity, Frankie Koehler,
police never caught him. The detective
reopened the case, logically reconstructed
an up-to-date family tree, obtained
subpoenas to trace calls, and found
Frankie hiding in California.
Against this powerful blend of
intuition and logic,
he was caught, confessed,
and sent to prison." [15]

A helpful process for integrating inner and reasoned knowing is termed "focusing" by its originator, philosopher-psychologist Eugene Gendlin, who built on the work of Carl Rogers at the University of Chicago. The process is valuable because it unlocks the body's wisdom to clarify what is wanted and needed. While Gendlin suggests the following focusing steps to bring inner knowing (signaled by a "felt shift") to conscious awareness, the process is not rigid. [16]

◆ *Get emotional distance from your problems.*

Gendlin advises: "If you want to smell a soup's aroma, get within sniffing distance, but keep your face out of the soup." To avoid the distracting pull of multiple issues, he suggests that you imagine placing all your concerns in bags outside your door and just bring back from your imagined hallway the one that, at this point in time, is most insistent.

_____

_____

_____

◆ *Notice your body signals.*

As you focus on your insistent issue, ask: What about it keeps me from feeling wonderful (or at peace, or productive) right now? Without effort, just notice your body's "felt sense." When you clarify what disturbs you or deadens your passion, your body may soften, tingle, or otherwise signal your attention.

_____

_____

_____

◆ *Identify the crux of your issue.*

What word, phrase, or image captures the essence of your concern? This step often stimulates fresh perspectives.

_____

_____

_____

◆ *Sense the totality.*

As you "keep company" with the whole focal issue, inquire: "What's the worst thing about this? Pat answers or defensive rationalizations may surface before a new perspective appears, ushered in by an "aha" or "felt shift.""

_____

_____

_____

◆ *Resolution.*

Inquire: "What needs to happen before this problem can be resolved?" Action steps emerge as you develop a responsive plan, explore consequences, and decide when, where, how, and with whom to proceed.

_____

_____

_____

Each of us can handle leadership issues more effectively and with greater satisfaction by harnessing the twin allies of inner wisdom to generate creative sparks, and reasoned logic to realize predictable outcomes.

While knowledge is always a vital component of leadership, leaders appreciate that people are more than what they know.

CHAPTER 4
MANAGING STRESS

If only I had known how long
I was going to live,
I would have taken
better care of myself.

—Anonymous

*T*he most visible sign of an effective leader is *self-care*—how well you manage your own life and your stress. Self-care is reflected in health, performance, teamwork, clarity, concentration, communication, and relationships. In this chapter, you will have the opportunity to examine sources of your stress, how well you are handling them, and relevant options to consider.

Some stress has as its source *external* pressures: budgets, difficult people, traffic, sex, deadlines, teenagers. Some stress is *self-generated*: perfectionism, a harsh inner critic, excessive worry, procrastination. *Stress is your response to perceived demands—external and self-generated—that tax your capacity to realize what most matters to you.*

The following inventory will help you determine ways in which stress impacts your life by assessing your reactivity, balancing mechanisms, and stress sources, and will suggest responsive strategies. One cautionary note: When responding to assessment questions, avoid the temptation to portray yourself as an angel (unless you have wings).

Assessing Your Stress

REACTIVITY

Respond to the following statements as you look back at the last month or so. If the statement refers to a situation that did *not* occur, insert "0." For each statement that occurred assign points using this guideline:

3 = Agree Strongly   **2 = Agree Moderately**

1 = Disagree Moderately   **0 = Disagree Strongly**

1. When things didn't go my way (the way I would have preferred), I got irritated. _____

2. When others got credit they didn't deserve, or were excessively self-promoting, I got annoyed. _____

3. I got impatient with one or more slow-speaking or slow-thinking people. _____

4. I often maneuvered my car (in a safe manner) around slower-moving vehicles to avoid wasting time. _____

5. I mentally compared my performance or effectiveness to others. _____

6. I took the successes or small victories of others as a challenge to out-perform them in the future. _____

Add your total scores for items 1 through 6.
This is your Subtotal A.   _____

BALANCE

As you look back at the last month or so, respond to the following situations that may have occurred. If the situation did *not* occur, insert "3." For each statement that occurred assign points using this guideline:

0 = Weekly or More Often   1 = About Every Other Week

2 = About Once a Month   3 = Rarely or Never

7. I engaged in creative or expressive activities
(such as art, music, writing, acting) outside
of work. _____

8. I devoted time to thinking about what really
matters to make my life feel more meaningful. _____

9. I engaged in a program of sustained
aerobic exercise. _____

0 = At Least Four Times a Week

1 = At Least Three Times a Week

10. I ate nutritiously, minimizing my intake of
sugars, processed, and high-cholesterol foods. _____

11. I received affection and caring support from
friends and family. _____

12. I was satisfied with the quality and frequency
of my sensual and sexual life. _____

13. I spent time meditating or otherwise
focusing my attention inwardly. _____

14. I felt serene in prayer or contemplation (such
as enjoying nature or appreciating the potential
for all people to connect in peaceful fellowship). _____

*Add your total scores for items 7 through 14.
This is your Subtotal B.* _____

STRESS SOURCES

Looking back (even years ago) to when a disturbing situation occurred, respond to the following situations indicating your *present level* of upset using this guideline:

3 = Feel Very Upset   *2 = Feel Moderately Upset*

1 = Feel Minor Level of Upset   *0 = Feel No Upset (or event never occurred)*

15. A person in my personal and/or work life is (or was) difficult. _____

16. My income, investments, or expenses greatly changed. _____

17. A person(s) close to me died, had a serious accident, illness, or an addiction. _____

18. I lost or expect to lose my job, or I feel badly for others who lost their jobs. _____

19. I am concerned with work problems (issues such as ethical behavior, career advancement, compensation, organizational changes). _____

20. One or more dependents present continuing problems. _____

21. I don't feel as healthy as I would like. _____

22. I don't have enough quality time with friends or family. _____

23. I feel a lack of control at work and/or in my personal life. _____

Add your total scores for items 15 through 23.
This is your Subtotal C. _____

Add Subtotals A ____ + B ____ + C ____ = ____ Your Score _____

Note: The author and publisher assume no liability and make no health claims for this Inventory.

Interpreting Your Stress Scores
Reactivity

People with high-level reactivity (also known as "Type A Behavior") respond to trying situations with a conditioned, or knee-jerk, reaction. If your score is above 12, you may feel pushed by one or more of the following feelings:

◆ Time Urgency—a compulsive need to rush;

◆ Aggressive Competitiveness—a pressing need to win irrespective of physical and emotional costs;

◆ Hostility—seeing others who get in your way as impediments to be removed or ignored.

Type A behavior is especially hard to change when "time urgency" is standard operating-procedure in your organization. Leadership mastery rests on recognizing:

1. On occasion, you may need to hurry and rushing is detrimental only when your inner driver creates an ongoing, unconscious behavioral pattern.

2. The human cost of mindless, aggressive rushing is high in terms of physical and emotional health.

3. Leaders who are not reactive—who remain centered under fire—are more likely to inspire the confidence of others.

To dramatize how different people can have vastly different inner experiences of identical external situations, S. I. Hayakawa offers this vignette:

> "Years ago, I noticed differences among operators on the Indiana Avenue streetcar line in Chicago—a street often blocked by badly parked cars and huge trailer trucks backing into warehouses and maneuvering in everybody's way. Some trolley operators seemed to expect to navigate Indiana Avenue without interruption. Every time they got blocked, they steamed up with rage, clanged their bells, and shouted at the truck drivers. At the end of each day, these operators must have been nervous wrecks; I can imagine them coming home jittery and hypertensive, a menace to their families. Other operators, however, sat with patience, calmly waiting or writing reports." [1]

Similar to the uptight Chicago trolley operators, here's a story a woman told at one of our leadership workshops.

> "My ex-husband, a high-powered Beverly Hills attorney, and I were on our long-deferred honeymoon in Venice. He phoned his secretary twice a day and handled business-as-usual from our bridal suite. One evening I suggested stopping for a cappuccino to enjoy a romantic sunset. He exploded: 'Don't you realize what time zone we are in? I barely have time to phone an important client.'"

Antidotes to reactive behavior include clarifying priorities, focusing attention on the quality of your relationships at home and at work, seeing possibilities for humor, and not taking yourself so seriously. (Example: "Is it true that after you took Dr. Kindler's training, you no longer had trouble reaching clear-cut decisions?" "Well, yes, and no.")

Balance

If your score is above 15, your life may be out of balance. If so, you may lack the *resilience* to bounce back from adverse circumstances and the inevitable pressures of daily living.

Balance requires attending to four interrelated human needs:

- *Physical*: Adequate exercise, wholesome nutrition, and daily relaxation.
- *Mental*: Taking time to pay attention to what really matters during the brief sojourn we call life.
- *Emotional*: Asking for, giving, and receiving emotional support from family and friends.
- *Spiritual*: Contemplative inquiry to heighten appreciation of life's gifts.

Good balance in these four domains manifests as:

- *Physical*: stamina, appropriate weight, flexibility, strength
- *Mental*: clarity, concentration, curiosity, creativity
- *Emotional*: mood stability, sensitivity, empathy
- *Spiritual*: serenity, compassion, inner peace

Stress Sources

If your score is above 18, you may want to pace yourself more gently and defer additional major commitments at this time. To the degree that you are feeling the heavy weight of adverse circumstances, consider the following:

- Can you change your perception?
- Can you constructively address the person(s) you perceive as contributing to your excessive stress?

◆ Can you find or create a more supportive environment or more satisfying relationships?

Managing Your Stress (2nd level heading)

When confronted with a stressful situation, rather than depend on an automatic, reflex reaction, consider choosing one of the following strategic responses for a more constructive resolution of the stress-inducing issue:

◆ Accept the source of stress by changing your perception
◆ Identify and address your perceived source of stress
◆ Exit or remove yourself from the situation

BEHAVIOR UNDER STRESS

Reflex Reaction	Fight	Flight	Freeze
	Attack or defend	Run from	Become paralyzed
Strategic Response	Address	Exit	Accept
	Deal with Issue	Choose to leave	Change perception

Accept by Changing Your Perception

While not always possible, if you can change how you look at a stressful situation—without changing its reality—you can reduce your stress. For example, when my son Alex was a teenager, he organized a band that practiced after school in his bedroom. When I got home from work, I was greeted with the ear-piercing sounds of drums, horns, and electric guitars. My shouts for the boys to shut the bedroom door only slightly muffled the cacophony. After some weeks of experiencing homecoming stress, I shifted my perception, telling myself: "Herb, what's your problem? Your son and his friends are not out on the street doing drugs; you know where they are and what they are doing." This shift in perception didn't totally eliminate my excessive stress, but it clearly reduced it.

Can you think of a stressful situation in which changing your perception without altering the situation reduced your stress level?

The identically enclosed space can be seen as:

Overwhelming

_____

_____

_____

_____

Identify and Address

As a young engineer in Oklahoma City, I was excited about all aspects of my job except one—contact with my boss. He rarely waited for me to finish sentences, continually interrupting me. When I finally confronted him, he replied: "Herb, you speak so slowly, I can't help but jump in." Some days later, I realized that my slow speaking pace started in childhood, rooted in auditory dyslexia. I often heard myself start a sentence with an out-of-sequence word. I discovered that I could avoid embarrassment, and catch errors before they popped out of my mouth simply by speaking slowly. Although I had outgrown this problem, I continued to speak slowly without realizing it. My lesson: The courage to address a perceived source of stress opens the opportunity to learn about oneself—particularly to see deeply ingrained dysfunctional habits.

Imprisoning

Just Right

Your perception matters.

Exit

The exit strategy for reducing stress is always an option. However, before you leave a situation with a history of ongoing stress, ask yourself: "What has been my contribution to the existence of continuing high stress levels?" Unless you understand how you were a party to, for example, interpersonal friction, a similar scenario may follow you into a future relationship.

Action Options

The ultimate measure of leadership is the capacity to translate strategy into behavior. Consider making a commitment to at least one of the following action options.

◆ Tell the reflection in your bathroom mirror each morning: "Don't take this person too seriously today."

◆ Celebrate, at home and at work, a small team victory, an obscure anniversary, a "nothing special" gathering—in the spirit of keeping your life fresh.

◆ Eat consciously and always while you are seated. (If you graze in the refrigerator, just open the door and pull up a chair.)

◆ If you have a harsh inner critic, send him or her on a long vacation.

◆ Call time out each day to ask: "What touched me today? What did I learn?"

Leading Honorably Tip: Assess Your Attitude

Your attitude is revealed in your words. If you have a pessimistic view of the world, your choice of words will no doubt sound negative. And negative word-choices do not fit with what General Colin Powell says about those who lead and the leadership attitudes they possess: "Optimism is a force-multiplier."

Take the following quiz to gain insight into your leadership language. For each statement, score yourself on the scale of 1 to 5 that most closely reflects your position on each statement, as follows:

1 = Not at all true of me

2 = Sometimes true of me

3 = True of me about half the time

4 = Often true of me

5 = Completely true of me

1. I "hold my tongue" when it would be easier to make a negative comment.   _____

2. I pride myself on remaining cool in tense situations.   _____

3. I mediate when others are having disputes.   _____

4. I refuse to engage in sarcasm.   _____

5. I accept change and interruptions good-naturedly.   _____

6. I listen to people without worrying about things I have to get done.   _____

7. I say positive things to and about others.   _____

8. In a situation involving extreme stress, time seems to slow down for me.   _____

9. I do not gossip.   _____

10. I "walk in the shoes of other people" before criticizing them.   _____

Total: _____

If your score was:

0–30: You have some work to do if you want to optimize your leadership language. You will find dozens of ideas in the following pages. And if you are serious about making the world a "kinder, gentler place," you can get started right now.

31–40: It is clear you are sensitive to the feelings of others. This sensitivity is the starting point for creating a more cooperative, harmonious culture, one in which both leadership and "follower-ship" can flourish. Continue what you are doing but also know there is room for even better interpersonal relationships.

PART II

STRATEGIC PLANNING

Strategy focuses attention
on those larger objectives and
processes worthy of
passionate commitment.

—Marilyn Ginsburg

CHAPTER 5

THE LEADERSHIP CONVERSATION

It has become urgent for
civilization that we share
the deep tacit process of
our consciousness and
think together.

—David Bohm

*W*ith increasing turbulence and complexity, leaders need to engage stakeholders in forthright conversation aimed at articulating creative opportunities. No longer is it the leader's role to unilaterally develop organizational strategy. The "new" leader recognizes that conversation is a medium with richer potential. No one person can have all "the answers;" all can be involved in finding promising possibilities.

Leadership conversations are not like bureaucratic committee meetings where people feel they are wasting time until they can get back to work. Leadership conversation *is* the work!

Leadership dialogue is inclusive, opening to relevant views of staff, customers, suppliers, community leaders, and consultants. When was the last time you invited customers to meet with you as a group to explore how mutual interests might be advanced?

Obstacles to group conversation are distrust of leader motives and the intrusion of dysfunctional ego needs—such as excessive need to control, be admired, or to prevail in argumentative debate. What facilitates coactive dialogue is shared purpose, common values, individual reflection, and relevant disclosure.

Sidestepping responsibility for developing one's own perspective reminds me of the time I asked a casual acquaintance if he liked a particular movie. The absence of personal reflection was stark. His response: "I don't know yet; I haven't had a chance to discuss it with my girlfriend."

Daily bombardment of information bits (data shrapnel) makes holistic thinking difficult. We visit specialists, read niche magazines, listen to television sound bites. Meaning—personal and professional—demands a larger context than these flying fragments. The goal of leadership conversation is to discover what is relevant and of value while building trust.

Historical Roots

Leadership conversation is at the heart of Native American council meetings and Quaker services where members sit in silence until an individual feels inspired to speak. That person then shares, without advocacy, the understanding or guidance that has "come through." Quakers refer to one another as "friends" capturing the feeling of equals respectful of one another's insights.

A systematic study of group conversation was launched at the end of World War II with the appearance of two experiments—Tavistock Study Group in England and National Training Laboratory (NTL) in the United States.[1] The programs, designed for executives interested in leadership and personal growth, were called T-groups, sensitivity training, and laboratory learning. The focus was (and remains—NTL Institute is still active) on self-awareness and authentic communication.

In contrast with typical corporate training, a facilitator-leader briefly introduces the process and sits back without further comment. With no "official" leader, structure, or agenda for the program, participants often feel discomfort. Here are comments of one participant, Charles Handy, professor at the London School of Business, reporting on his first NTL experience in the United States.

"I was nervous. As an outsider from abroad,
I decided to keep quiet and watch others discuss a
plan. At one point, someone suggested we
check impressions as follows: 'Put your name
on a piece of paper and pass it around. We each will
write a word or phrase describing how we see you.
When all the papers have gone around, we will each
unfold our own and find the feedback comments.'

"I had nothing to lose. I had said nothing
and expected to get back an empty piece of paper.
But I had a full complement of comments. Snob.
Patronizing. Stuck up. Unapproachable.
Superior and more.

They had dumped all their stereotypes
of the British
onto me, I jumped to my feet,
red-faced and furious, stung into speech
ending with: '...and I'm not even British.
I'm Irish.' They laughed. I forgave them.
It was me speaking, not a silent stereotype." [2]

Leadership dialogue fails when based on assumptions and expectations. Conversely, notice how forgiving and cooperative others are when you say your truth and allow yourself to be vulnerable. The challenge for the leader-facilitator is to help group members express themselves without hiding behind roles—and by *talking with* each other rather than *presenting to* each other.

Leadership conversation is not debate. In debate, like a Ping-Pong match, ideas are batted back and forth to win points. In dialogue, the aim is win-win by collaboratively seeking shared meaning and common understanding.

Dialogue is nourished by mutual respect and defeated when members feel ignored or discounted. Here's a personal experience that dramatized this point for me.

For almost two years, my wife and I met monthly with six others who shared professional interests. Our meetings were stimulating and fun until the day Jonathan announced that he invited his friend Blake to join our group.

With obvious embarrassment, Anna urged the group not to accept Blake as a member. She confessed to an extramarital affair with Blake some years before. Anna's current husband, also a group member, added:

"Jonathan, my comfort level would benefit from not admitting Blake, at least, not at this time."

Unmoved, Jonathan said he did not intend to withdraw his invitation, adding: "This is not the big deal you two are making it into. You are both being childishly over-sensitive." Anna's husband countered with some colorful language around the theme of Jonathan being an insensitive idiot.

Disrespect is not the soil in which group conversation flourishes. It takes root when nourished by compassion and good will. It blossoms when differences are sensitively *resolved* (harmonized) or *dissolved* (seen from other levels as facets of the same unity).

People connect in ways that are satisfying and productive only in the presence of empathy and respect. Jonathan's unilateral, closed-minded position and lack of compassion probably reflected his ego-need to look influential to his friend Blake. That evening was the group's last meeting.

A lesson in keeping an open mind is reflected in this story by spiritual leader and former Harvard professor, Ram Das.[3]

In Russia, some centuries ago, a poor farmer's
son left the corral gate open and
their only horse ran away. A neighbor
expressed sympathy to which the farmer replied:
"You never know."

The horse returned the next day leading
two wild horses to the barn.
The farmer's response to the neighbor's
congratulations was:
"You never know."

When the son attempted to ride
one of the wild horses,
he was thrown and broke a leg.
(I was among some 500 people in the
audience when Ram Das
invited us to join him in saying
to the sympathy-giving neighbor:
"You never know.")

Finally, Cossack recruiters arrived and
excused the son from being
conscripted into the army
because of his injury.
The audience shouted in unison:
"You never know!"

The story serves as a reminder to remain receptive to alternative
possibilities. In summary, in the most productive leadership

conversations, participants ask themselves the following questions that you, the reader, can also consider:

- Am I trying to impress anyone?
- Am I hiding my vulnerability by guarding relevant, but potentially embarrassing, information?
- Do I want to be seen as a loyal team player (rather than express dissident views)?
- Do I want to keep a "low profile"?
- Am I trying to fill what feels like an awkward silence?

By keeping mutual inquiry focused on the group's common purpose and maintaining sensitive self-awareness, leaders inspire others to contribute the unique gifts that move organizations forward.

Leading Honorably Tip: Persuade by Listening

Statesman Dean Rusk believed in persuading well by listening well. When you truly attend to the words of another person, you are "saying" many things with your honorable behavior. You are saying that:

- The other person is worth listening to.
- You are patient enough not to interrupt with ideas of your own.
- The other person deserves your respect.
- Followers may have ideas as good as your own, even if you are the recognized leader.
- You are not a control freak who must have everything done according to your own plan.

In short, you are persuading others that you are trustworthy, open-minded, and patient—three traits that leaders have in abundance.

How Well Do You Listen?

Circle the numbers for the following questions to which you can answer "Yes."

1. Do you watch facial expressions of others as you talk with them?
2. Do your expressions show sincere interest?
3. Do you maintain eye contact throughout exchanges?
4. Do you give feedback to show you are interested? (If so, how?)
5. Do you deliberately avoid interrupting others as they speak?
6. Do you maintain a comfortable distance from others?
7. Do you paraphrase to check your understanding?
8. Do you inquire about the feeling behind the words?
9. Do you work at not finishing sentences for other people?
10. Do you show respect for the opinions of others who disagree with your viewpoint?

If you possess the courage typically associated with leaders, give this list to five other people and ask them to answer yes or no to these questions about your listening behaviors. If their answers disagree with yours, do not become defensive. Instead, consider ways to improve your listening skills so you can, correspondingly, improve your language skills.

CHAPTER 6
DEALING WITH DISAGREEMENT

Leaders transform potentially
divisive conflict and
defensiveness into learning.

—Peter Senge

*L*eadership is fueled by disagreement. Your challenge is to harness energy generated by conflicting views to clarify issues, build trust, initiate needed change, correct misunderstandings, and stimulate learning. In contrast, poorly handled disagreement dissipates energy, stifles creative dissent, polarizes positions, seeds rivalry, triggers bickering, and inflames feelings.

This chapter suggests how to deal with disagreement using four core principles:

1. Don't take yourself too seriously
2. Don't grip your position too tenaciously.
3. Listen, really listen.
4. Use a conflict intervention strategy that opens creative possibilities and builds relationship bridges.

Hold Differences Lightly

Abraham Lincoln is a wonderful role model of someone who didn't take himself too seriously. One story Lincoln told on himself was the time he was approached by an elderly woman who gave him this gratuitous advice:

"Mr. Lincoln, you should not run for reelection.
You really are too ugly."

"It's too late to back out now. I've already committed
to run again. But maybe you can suggest how I could
deal with this ugliness problem."

"Well, yes. You might stay home more often."

Oliver Cromwell, in a letter to the General Assembly of the Church of Scotland in 1650, presented an impassioned plea to leave room for disagreement and continued inquiry: "I beseech you, in the bowels of Christ, think it possible you may be mistaken."

Listen with Presence

Most people take for granted they are good listeners. Check this assumption for yourself by asking a friend to read the following short story to you—only once. When you have heard to story, respond to five questions. Don't take notes.

A salesman just turned off the lights in the store when
a man appeared and demanded money. The owner
opened the cash register. The contents of the cash
register were scooped up and the man ran away. A
member of the police force was promptly notified.

After you listen to the story, respond to the following questions by circling either TRUE or FALSE. *Don't look back to review the story.*

1. The person demanding money was a man.

        TRUE   FALSE

2. The person who opened the cash register was the owner.

        TRUE   FALSE

3. A man appeared after the owner had turned off the store lights.

        TRUE   FALSE

4. The story contains a series of events in which four persons are referred to.

        TRUE   FALSE

5. The man did not specifically demand money.

        TRUE   FALSE

In workshops with typically 25 participants, despite ideal listening conditions—where I have everyone's attention, announce that questions will follow the story, and I speak loudly—only one or two people answer all five questions correctly.

[Answers: (1) True; (2) True; (3) False; (4) True; (5) False.]

Why don't most participants get the facts of this simple story straight? Did you?

Here's how participants explain this anomaly:

♦ There was no *redundancy*—if I lost my concentration, even for a moment, I missed pertinent information that wasn't repeated.

♦ The story was *boring*—I wasn't motivated to pay close attention.

♦ There was no opportunity to ask *questions*.

♦ No *context* was given by which to understand the significance of the story.

Reversing these feedback comments suggests how to improve oral communication:

- ◆ Build some "creative repetition" into your comments.
- ◆ Say how you intend to address the interests of your audience.
- ◆ Invite questions.
- ◆ Provide context for your remarks.

The value of context, can be appreciated by the following scenario: [1]

> There is a man at home.
>
> The man is wearing a mask.
>
> There is a man coming home.

What is going on here in this seemingly disjointed narrative that appears vaguely related to a home burglary? Only after context is provided—that is, only after you know that the action takes place within the framework of a *baseball game*, can you understand that the man at home is a baseball catcher who will try to tag out the runner before he reaches home plate.

Plan a Strategic Intervention

In addition to maintaining your sense of humor and a receptive attitude, choose a *strategy* for dealing with differences. After combing a variety of disciplines—management, psychology, political science, negotiation, drama, sociology, public administration, and law—I found nine strategies used to resolve disagreement.[2]

I also discovered two threads running through all nine strategies: How *firm or flexible*, and how *engaged or impersonal* to be when dealing with conflicting views. The following graph illustrates the relationship of these factors.

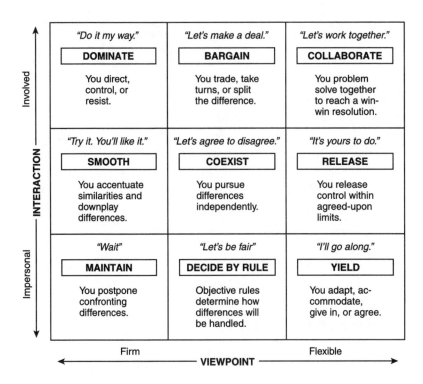

Assume you are dealing with *interdependent* relationships that really matter. That is, those involved depend on each other for completing a task, getting satisfaction, or both. Stated another way, we aren't concerned with resolving the type of situation in which a sports fan disagrees with an umpire's call.

Like playing golf with a full set of clubs, following is a full repertoire of strategies for dealing with disagreement.

Maintain: Table Action for Now
Firm Position/Low Engagement

Strategy—Postpone confronting differences while maintaining the status quo; appropriate only on an interim basis.

Why use this strategy?

 ◆ You lack relevant information

 ◆ Emotions are out of control

- Higher priority issues require your attention
- You need time to enlist support

Smooth: Grease the Skids
Firm Position/Moderate Engagement

Strategy—Accentuate the positive aspects of your position and downplay its limitations.

Why use this strategy?

- To create interest in your ideas
- To gain resources to test your ideas
- To follow Mary Poppins' advice: "A spoonful of sugar helps the medicine go down"

Dominate/Direct: Do It
Firm Position/High Engagement

Strategy—You unilaterally direct, control, or constrain action.

Why use this strategy?

- To deal with emergencies requiring prompt action
- To enforce rules (such as displaying security badges or wearing safety glasses)
- To direct novices in tasks unfamiliar to them

A problem associated with excessive use of this strategy is its tendency to evoke *counter-domination*. For example, here's a radio transcript allegedly released by the chief of U.S. Naval Operations:

<u>Station #1</u>: Divert your course 15 degrees to the North to avoid a collision.

<u>Station #2</u>: Recommend you divert YOUR course 15 degrees to the South to avoid a collision.

Station #1: This is the Captain of a U.S. Navy ship.
I say again, divert YOUR Course.

Station #2: No. I say again, you divert YOUR course.

Station #1: THIS IS THE AIRCRAFT CARRIER ENTERPRISE.
WE ARE A LARGE WARSHIP OF THE US NAVY. DIVERT
YOUR COURSE NOW!

Station #2: This is the Puget Sound lighthouse.
It's your call.

Decide by Rule: Let's Be Fair
Moderately Firm/Low Engagement

Strategy—An objective rule is applied such as majority-rule voting, seniority, lottery, test scores, Robert's Rules of Order, a coin flip, or an arbitration ruling

Why use this strategy?

♦ Multiple solutions are equally appropriate (such as deciding among several feasible dates for holding a company picnic; or choosing one person among several equally qualified candidates for overtime work)

♦ You want to resolve an issue quickly and have those involved perceive the resolution process as fair and impartial

Coexist: Agree to Disagree
Moderately Firm/Moderate Engagement

Strategy—Two parties agree to test alternative plans for a specific time period. They also agree on criteria for assessing the merits of each plan. At the end of the allotted time, they choose the action option that best meets the criteria they set and agree to work cooperatively using the preferred plan.

Why use this interim strategy?

◆ To provide time for one party to demonstrate the superiority of his/her position

◆ To gain energetic implementation of the better action plan

Bargain: Half a Loaf Is Better Than None
Moderately Firm/High Engagement

Strategy—An exchange process to decide what each gives and each receives.

Why use this strategy?

◆ Both parties believe they can gain more through give and take interaction using offers and counter offers than by "walking away"

Yield: Discretion Is the Better Part of Valor
High Flexibility/Low Engagement

Strategy—You support the views of others despite disagreeing with them.

Why use this strategy?

◆ The issue is more serious for another person than for you (For example, the need is more acute for an office mate with asthma to get the window seat that you also prefer)

◆ The other person has far more experience and expertise than you

This excerpt from *Love in the Time of Cholera* by Nobel prize winning author, Gabriel Garcia Marquez, illustrates the value of yielding to advance domestic tranquility.[3] The narrative takes place in the home of an aristocratic Colombian family in the late 1800s. Despite several live-in servants, stocking the master bathroom with such personal supplies as soap and toilet paper is a task reserved for the owner's wife. One morning, Dr. Urbino complains:

> "I've been bathing for almost a week
> without any soap." His angered wife defends
> herself by lying: "Well, I've bathed every day and
> there's always been soap." For the next three months,
> each time they tried to resolve the conflict, they
> inflamed their feelings even more. Dr. Urbino chose
> to sleep in his study until his wife was ready to admit
> there had been no soap in the bathroom.
>
> After four months had gone by, he lay down in their
> bed while she showered and he fell asleep. She shook
> him by the shoulder to remind him that he was sup-
> posed to go to the study, but he felt so comfortable in
> their featherbed that he preferred to capitulate. "Let
> me stay here," he said, "There was soap."

P.S. After 30 years of marriage, when my wife and I find ourselves embroiled in a mindless argument, one of us generally
has the presence to "wake" us with these code words: "Yes dear,
there was soap."

Release: Try Your Wings
High Flexibility/Moderate Engagement

Strategy—Even though you are in a position of authority (as a
manager or as a parent), you accept the views of a direct report
or maturing child. You may impose limits (such as a budget,
deadline, or curfew).

Why use this strategy?

- ◆ You want the other person to develop their own re-
  sourcefulness, initiative, and self-confidence on an issue
  of relatively minor consequence

Collaborate: Win-Win Problem Solving
High Flexibility/High Engagement

Strategy—You jointly create a mutually beneficial resolution, disclosing all relevant information.

Why use this strategy?

- ◆ To gain high energy commitment to an action plan on a significant issue
- ◆ To build high trust, cooperative relationships
- ◆ To share insights and gain skill in participating in leadership conversations

What passes for collaboration and gives it a bad name, in Thomas Jefferson's words:

"Too many are afflicted with impatience for any logic that is not their own—particularly when the group [Congress] is a body of lawyers whose trade it is to question everything, yield nothing, and talk by the hour."[4]

Please review the following case as you look in at one couple's experience of dealing with discord.

Case Study: The Bickersons

George and Martha, after three years of marriage, have a heated exchange.

> GEORGE: I don't believe my ears! You've waited until now, the last possible moment, to tell me you're enrolling in college for the coming semester. Don't you think you should have at least consulted me first? How come you suddenly have to be Ms. Martha Coed?

MARTHA: Don't get so worked up. We still have a couple of days before I have to mail in my enrollment forms.

GEORGE: I don't get it. You haven't been inside a classroom in five years. Suddenly, it's a top priority for you to get more education. You know I'm struggling to get my business off the ground; and you know I've been counting on your salary during my startup phase. What's going on?

MARTHA: Look George, it's no big secret. If you had been listening to me, you would know that I am totally bored with my job. I need a change. My boss is more supportive and understanding than you. She says that with a master's degree I can get a really interesting and better paying job.

GEORGE: It's the timing that makes no sense. If you keep your job, two years from now, I'll have a thriving business operation that will generate enough income so I can enroll you in the best college in the city.

MARTHA: I can't take it for another two years. Don't you understand that? And all you do is work-work-work seven days a week. There's no fun left in our marriage.

GEORGE: I'm working 12 hours a day for our future. I need to buy new equipment to be competitive. Just hang in and the business will start making money.

MARTHA: George, I want a life!

How would you continue this conversation?

_____

_____

_____

What strategy is appropriate?

_____

_____

_____

Case Study Discussion

This marriage is in trouble. Totally absent is even a glimmer of "lightness"—the lubricant for all interpersonal problem solving. Also missing is empathic listening. George seems so obsessed by his business that he hasn't heard Martha's pain—apparently for some time. Even in the brief dialogue, he misses her plea for more together time and a more balanced lifestyle. The appropriate strategy to manage this discord is "collaboration" where mutual problem solving is desperately needed.

To resolve any disagreement constructively, a starting point is clarity about objectives. We can guess that what is wanted (if not too late) is (1) a loving relationship, and (2) professional satisfaction for both partners. However, instead of a collaborative approach, the couple is engaged in a power struggle. Martha has delayed informing George about her graduate program plans; George assumes ownership not only of the business and Martha's salary, but also, he thinks he is in charge of financing Martha's education.

If the couple can get past their power jousting, creative possibilities they could collaboratively develop include:

◆ Martha might consider choosing her graduate education in business—getting an MBA degree—so she and George could work together as equal partners.

- Financially, George might raise capital by seeking investors; he could see if he qualifies for a small business loan. Martha might work part-time; she might seek a job at a college where she could take courses tuition-free or work part-time.

- To have time together for intimate relating, Martha and George could plan a weekly "date night".

- To stimulate other creative options, each (particularly George) could pose the question: What would I do if I were not married?

By addressing disagreement with sensitive respect, the range of what is collectively possible expands. Vision and values are clarified. People, organizations, and societies move closer to living in a peaceful, productive, and satisfying world.

Leading Honorably Tip: Play the Games Worth Playing

You may prefer to avoid organizational politics, but being politically savvy can often spell the difference between stalemate and success. To make a difference, to assume leadership, to bring about improvements in your workplace, you will find politics an unavoidable aspect of being effective.

Still, there is a possible downside to making politics work for you: As you contemplate how best to get things done—whether or not you are in charge of those things—you may feel you are strategizing to the point of manipulation.

Persuasion or Manipulation?

To clarify the distinction between unethical and ethical manipulation, ask yourself: If I succeed in having things turn out the way I want them to, will others profit as much as I will? If the answer is no, chances are the effort is negative manipulation. But if benefits will accrue to several people or to the organization as well as to you, then your political maneuvering is designed to serve the common good. And then you are using influence as it should be used.

Case Study: Politics Is Not a "Four-Letter Word"

In this case study, four co-workers have been operating as a team for the last six months on a benchmarking study they are ready to launch, pending approval from the executive committee. Tim, Sue, Chynna, and Whitney are meeting one last time to plan how they will make the presentation to the committee. What follows are each of their proposals for the presentation. Determine which one strategy you believe will most influence the others to accept it.

TIM: I think we should be planning a contingency strategy. There's a strong possibility, you know, that they won't fund this. So I propose that we continue meeting every month, revise our original proposal, and keep on submitting it until they say, "Go for it."

SUE: I agree that we have a limited chance of gaining approval right now. But if they do say no, then I think we should engage in some informal benchmarking. We can gather data, and then if further or formal studies are warranted, we can resubmit our proposal, using the data we've gathered to validate our proposal.

CHYNNA: There seems to be some doubt about getting the approval we need to move forward. This is what I think we should do. Let's present our proposal as a modified pilot project. It will take less time for us to prepare it today if it's a modified version. And more important, I think the committee will be more willing to fund something that is limited in scope. If we can get approval on the sequential steps, one at a time, we are more likely to win the committee over than if we ask for the whole plan to be approved at once. And while the pilot study is going on, we can learn more about the committee members to see what appeals we can make to them. We can determine what's in it for them.

WHITNEY: Ah, the old WIIFM—What's In It For Me—factor. It does have some merit, finding out what they are interested in and appealing to them on those interests. It has merit, but here's what I think we should do. Polish our presentation in the time we have left today. Make the presentation on Thursday as planned. If it is rejected, ask them why. Then we can decide if we want to pursue fixing it up for resubmission.

◆ Whose plan did you select as the most feasible?

_____

_____

_____

◆ Whose plan would you say is the most political?

_____

_____

_____

◆ Of all the people you know, who would you say is the most political?

_____

_____

_____

- Ask that person which of these four options he or she would have chosen and why.

Sometimes when a team is experiencing gridlock, it helps to bring in an outside opinion to ease team members through decisions to be made.

Chapter 7
Taking Risks

A life without adventure is likely
to be unsatisfying, but a life in
which adventure is allowed to take
whatever form it will, is likely to
be short.

—Bertrand Russell

*I*n turbulent times, a central leadership challenge is to determine when risk taking is warranted. The cost, even of carefully calculated risk, is occasional failure.

For example, in one company, a technical specialist misjudged development time to ready a new product for market. The cost of not getting the product to market first was estimated to cost the firm about $100,000. When the manager asked the involved staff member—in a matter-of-fact tone—what she had learned from the experience, her surprise was reflected in the question: "You mean I'm not fired?" "Hell, no. How could we even think of firing you? We've just invested $100,000 in your education."

In addition to making corporate life safe for risk taking, leaders involve themselves in conversations concerning which risks to take, pass, or modify. The following four factors offer guidance in this determination:

- An individual's or group's propensity to take risks
- Potential for gain
- Vulnerability to loss
- Uncertainty

Assessing these four factors suggests risk level and how the likelihood of realizing a favorable outcome can be improved.

Risk Taking Propensity

Consider the following questions for insight into your own bias to engage or avoid risk.

Do you prefer:

- ◆ Security over adventure?   ____ yes   ____no
- ◆ Structure over improvisation?   ____ yes   ____no
- ◆ Stability over change?   ____ yes   ____no
- ◆ Comfort over stimulation?   ____ yes   ____no
- ◆ "Fitting in" over "standing out"? ____ yes   ____no

If you responded to the checklist with more "yes's" than "no's," consider the possibility that you have a risk-averse orientation and tend to choose more conservative options with lower potential for both gain and loss. Conversely, if you responded with more "no's," you prefer risk seeking, choosing more radical options with greater potential for gain and loss.

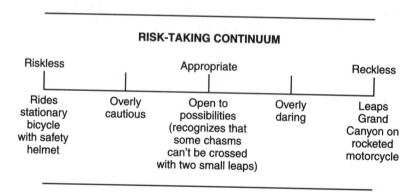

RISK-TAKING CONTINUUM

Riskless		Appropriate		Reckless
Rides stationary bicycle with safety helmet	Overly cautious	Open to possibilities (recognizes that some chasms can't be crossed with two small leaps)	Overly daring	Leaps Grand Canyon on rocketed motorcycle

Risk aversion and risk seeking are not absolute; the bias can shift depending both on group dynamics and specific situations. I know one man, a physician, who, during winter vacations, has a helicopter drop him off at remote, snow-covered mountaintops on skis to add an element of adventure. Yet, when it comes to financial investing, he is ultra-cautious. An extreme risk orientation is obvious. For example, a daredevil motorcycle stunt driver, Evel Knievel, attempted (unsuccessfully) to leap across the Snake River Canyon in Idaho on a rocket propelled bike. (He buffered his risk by wearing a parachute.) At the other end of the risk spectrum would be a person who pedals a stationary exercise bicycle wearing a safety helmet. For the vast majority between these extremes, examining risk propensity is a helpful exercise in self-awareness.

Research suggests that risk avoiders, compared with risk seekers, are more pessimistic about likely outcomes, want more information, more control, lower stakes, shared responsibility, and a detailed exit plan from risky situations should they turn sour. Risk seekers, in contrast, are more optimistic, impulsive, and thrive on high stakes risk. Generally, more effective decisions are made by groups whose members reflect a range of risk-taking orientations. [1]

Historical examples of excessive leader-influence (and group self-censorship) include the ill-fated Bay of Pigs Cuban invasion after which President John F. Kennedy asked himself: "How could I have been so stupid (as to agree to implement the CIA's high-risk plan)?" Similarly, why did Lyndon Johnson keep escalating the Vietnam War with its tragic consequences? In each case, the voices of more temperate colleagues, who might have argued against these ill-advised, risky decisions, were silent. [2]

The lesson: Do not allow social pressure (*groupthink*) to muzzle dissent. Use group conversation to articulate the risks and develop creative alternatives. Seek counsel from teams whose members reflect a balanced risk-taking orientation, and who are willing to express unpopular views.

Maximize Potential for Gain

◆ *Proactive Orientation.* A proactive stance can improve
the odds of realizing gains. For example, the value of
my home is enhanced by a lovely private patio. Imagine
my concern seeing a portable toilet on my neighbor's
lawn, signaling construction of a second story. Rather
than risk having my neighbor gain a choice view of my
wife's sunbathing activities, I proactively offered to pay
for any architectural design changes that would assure our continued privacy—such as use of glass brick
or clerestory windows. (I stopped short of suggesting
stained-glass windows.)

◆ *Learning from Experience.* Basic to improving your potential for gain is a lessons-learned program. Boeing, for
example, commissioned an employee group to review
successes and failures associated with introducing its
737 and 747 planes. The team compiled literally hundreds of "lessons learned" that appeared applicable to
future projects. As a result, the 767 start-up yielded the
most successful, error-free launch in Boeing's history.[3]

◆ *Autonomy.* Granting hands-off independence to highly
creative individuals and teams can pay off with long-
term gains. IBM Fellows, for example, are granted
significant periods of time off from assigned tasks to
pursue projects of their own choosing. They receive
full funding, support personnel, space, and equipment
and are left to their own initiative. Result: In addition
to breakthrough innovation and a motivational boost,
IBM Fellows have contributed substantially to company
income from invention licensing that currently totals
over $1 billion per year.

Reduce Vulnerability to Loss

To minimize exposure to loss, consider these options:

- *Diversify.* The stock-in-trade of financial advisers is portfolio diversification—balancing type of assets— stocks, bonds, real estate, money market; balancing large, medium, and small cap stocks; and balancing such sectors as high tech, cyclical industries, and commodities.

- *Safety Net.* If you have to bail out, how can you cushion your fall (such as an employee severance pay package for high-risk projects)? Can you place a stop-loss order on volatile investments? Have you a contingency Plan B?

- *Buffers.* Some banks use bulletproof, clear plastic enclosures and surveillance cameras to protect tellers. Others use metal detectors.

- *Pilot Tests.* Small-scale prototype testing, focus groups, gradual phase-in, and regional trials offer a relatively low-cost perspective on proposal validity.

- *Multiple Scenarios.* By developing worst-case scenarios, fresh alternatives can be stimulated and recovery plans designed.

- *Alliances.* Especially where stakes are high, consider joint ventures to guard against substantial losses, especially for innovative research. Such an alliance was formed by two rival automakers, Ford and DaimlerChrysler, who teamed with the Canadian firm, Ballard Power Systems, to pursue high-cost automotive fuel-cell research.

Minimize Uncertainty

- *More Information.* Can you delay action to let relevant information unfold? Or, will waiting for more definitive information give competitors a significant, even irreversible, advantage? Often, the sense of urgency is illusory. People with a risk-seeking bias want quick action. (Fire—Ready—Aim.)

♦ *Greater Control.* Don't expect total control—a strategy that usually is self-defeating. For example, when the Hunt Brothers of Dallas tried to control the price of silver by cornering bullion, they lost over $1 billion in the 1980 silver market crash.

♦ *Simulation.* One tactic to reduce risk, such as in the difficult process of employee hiring, is to observe a candidate actually working the job. The Assessment Center concept, pioneered by Development Dimensions International, simulates real job activities with a work agenda in a mock office equipped with computer and phone. Job behavior is recorded on video for later review.

♦ *Legal/Financial Protection.* During the process of selling my publishing business, we tentatively agreed on a price to be paid over five years. However, my attorney noted: "The buyer's financial health looks good now. But, how can we be sure payments will continue should he suffer a major illness or financial loss?" To protect against this vulnerability, our final agreement provided a line-of-credit that guaranteed full, timely payments by his bank unrelated to the buyer's fiscal viability. For added protection, we reduced the payment period to three years, and required the buyer to secure a life insurance policy naming me as beneficiary.

♦ *Candor.* You learn from experience only when you can talk candidly about your errors. During a high-level strategy meeting in which I participated, the CEO of an international restaurant chain reminded his executives: "We don't tolerate mediocrity." On learning that four of his popular restaurants in New York City ran out of paper napkins, he exploded, repeating his we-don't-tolerate-mediocrity mantra. The "guilty" manager was so chagrined she later ordered a two-year supply of napkins and rented warehouse space to store them. A more risk-friendly leader—where mistakes are grist for the learning mill—doesn't tempt employees to avoid embarrassment through ultra-conservative or even unethical behavior.

Case Study: Lonely at the Top

Paul Price is CEO of Mayco, a *Fortune 500* corporation. Since his wife died two years ago, Price has felt lonely and isolated. Recently, however, at his club, he met Ralph Stone, a member with whom he now regularly plays golf and whose companionship he enjoys.

This morning, Mayco's public relations director, Jane Osgood, visits Paul in his office. Jane seats herself and after brief casual comments, says:

JANE: Paul, did you know that Ralph Stone gave you as a character reference when he submitted a bid to the Larson Company for some work as a financial consultant?

PAUL: Yes, he asked if he could use my name and I said, "Of course."

JANE: I have unpleasant news. The human resources people at Larson did a background check on Mr. Stone and learned that he is an ex-convict who was convicted for insider trading. To Stone's credit, when asked if he had any relevant negative information to disclose, he told them about serving prison time.

PAUL: I can't fully take in what you are saying. Ralph Stone seems like such a fine person, interesting, full of creative ideas. I'm shocked.

JANE: What is clear to me is the need to distance yourself from Stone. Continuing a close relationship would be risky. The media loves this type of story and publicity might dramatize how Stone duped you. The publicity could shake investor confidence and affect Mayco's stock price.

I hope I am not being intrusive into your private affairs, but let me risk advising you to stop seeing Ralph Stone.

What action would you advise CEO Paul Price to take?

_____

_____

_____

Why?

_____

_____

_____

Case Study Discussion

Jane Osgood suggested two options to Paul Price: an either/or choice—presenting two undesirable action possibilities—either end the friendship, or sacrifice innocent stockholders.

Woody Allen pokes fun at either/or reasoning, using this example: "Either we can take the path that leads to endless misery; or, we can take the other path that leads to human extinction. Let us pray we will have the wisdom to choose wisely."

What would be a creative alternative to ending the friendship—an alternative worth the risk of exposing innocent stockholders to potential losses? Price could consider launching a community-wide study to examine when it is appropriate for organizations to hire and train ex-convicts. Ralph Stone might be appointed as project advisor. Instead of concern about negative leaks to the media, Price could call a press conference to announce the project and Stone's appointment.

PART III

ENERGIZING

PERFORMANCE

Leadership closes the gap between
possibility and performance.

—Rosabeth Moss Kanter

Chapter 8
Leading Change

We must be the change we
wish to see in the world.

—Gandhi

*D*uring a business trip to London, associates took my wife and me to dinner at the Reform Club. I learned that this institution had been a wellspring of radical ideas in Britain two centuries earlier. We were treated to the Club's ornate splendor that included a lavish, six-course dinner. Afterward, I was ushered into a gender-segregated lounge to discuss business over cigars and port wine. Despite its apt name when founded, the Reform Club had become traditional and stuffy.

How can you and the organizations in which you have a leadership role remain relevant and vibrant? This chapter examines two core strategies: incremental change within an *existing* system, and seeding a *new* system with transformational change.

Climbing the S-Curve

Nature offers familiar examples of exponential growth that in time is arrested by physical constraints—such as sunflower seedlings in containers, the rabbit population in Australia, and fruit flies in a screen-capped jar. As fruit flies master the mating dance, offspring multiply until the system (jar) inhibits further growth. This process roughly traces an S-curve—*take-off phase, rapid growth*, and *stability or decline.* The fruit-fly jar is both a literal and metaphoric expression of systems (such as the rigid boundaries of bureaucracies) that inhibit or block further growth.

This three-phase change-pattern appears in both natural and people-created systems. Science philosopher, Derek de Solla Price, pointed out that the S-curve is ubiquitous with deep historical roots.

If you graph the number of universities founded in the European Middle Ages, you see a sigmoid curve starting slowly in 950, growing exponentially at first and falling away slowly by the beginning of the Renaissance in 1450.

Price observed that growth need not plateau—a second S-curve, with new potential, could be triggered, based on a *new system*. He noted that rapid growth was renewed after the nature of the university radically changed (moving the locus of control from students to faculty). He concluded:

The lesson of renewed exponential growth is obvious; the old order began to die on its feet and, in so doing, allowed a new concept of the university to arise. [1]

Still later, after the Renaissance-university building spree leveled, new paradigms fueled fresh interest that took the form of government-funded universities and community colleges (moving control from faculty to administrators).

Where leaders seek growth , it can be encouraged by climbing a *series* of S-curves using two strategies sequentially: *transformational* and *incremental* change.

Transformational Change

Transformational change alters a conceptual framework. Such change requires leadership because it threatens vested interests, challenges the competence of incumbents and, inevitably, bumps up against resistance. Despite these obstacles, its potential for renewal is compelling.

Transformational change prompted John Dewey to write:

**Every radical thinker puts some portion
of an apparently stable world in peril
and no one can predict what will emerge in its place.** [2]

James Baldwin also captured the power of radical change:

**Any real (transformational) change implies
the breakup of the world as one has always known it,
the loss of all that gave one an identity, the end of And
at such a moment, unable to see and not
daring to imagine what the future will now bring
forth, one clings to what one knew, or thought one
knew; to what one possessed, or dreamed one possessed.Yet, it is only when a person is able, without
bitterness or self-pity, to surrender a dream long
cherished or a privilege long possessed that
one is set free—sets oneself free—for higher
dreams, greater privileges.** [3]

The power of transformation and the need to disidentify with the status quo are dramatized in this Sufi teaching story, retold by Indries Shah.

From its source in a far-off mountain range, a stream
passed through every kind of countryside until it
reached the desert sands. Just as it had crossed every
other barrier, the stream tried to cross the desert. But
the sand, with its insatiable thirst, swallowed it.
Now a hidden voice whispered:

"The wind crosses the desert and so can you. By
hurtling yourself at the sand in your own accustomed
way, you will never get across. You must allow the
wind to carry you to your destination."

This idea was not acceptable to the stream. It had
never been absorbed and did not want to lose its
identity. Finally, after much anguish, the stream
raised its vapor into the arms of the wind,
which gently bore it upwards,
letting it fall softly as it reached a mountain and
re-formed into a new stream. [4]

Transformational leaders harness the winds that bring a change
in *kind*, not just in *degree*; they move away from "that's how
we do things around here;" they seek *revitalization*, not refine-
ment.

Incremental Change

Once leaders pursue a radical change that triggers the start of
a new S-curve, it is sustained by several step-by-step changes
within the emergent system. For example, suppose you head
a business that launched an innovative product line and you
want your operation to climb a healthy growth S-curve. Rather
than introduce several revolutionary changes in rapid-fire
succession, a more cost-effective strategy is to develop a series

of incremental changes. In a business context, these changes might take form as expanded advertising, product rebates, low interest customer loans, product design refinements, or longer warranty periods. In other words, your aim is to ride the crest created by transformational change (while your research department is filling the pipeline with innovative ideas for future implementation).

Public administration professor Charles Lindblom, in his article, "The Science of Muddling Through," suggests where incremental change is the preferred strategy.

Democracies change their policies almost entirely through incremental adjustments. Policy does not move in leaps and bounds, but shifts largely through a series of relatively small changes. Because policies being considered are like present and past policies, administrators can claim some insight. Wise policy makers hope to avoid unanticipated consequences by proceeding through a succession of incremental changes. They need not attempt big jumps toward goals that would require predictions beyond anyone's knowledge. A decision is only one step, one that if successful can be followed by another, and a past error can be remedied quickly.[5]

Sometimes incremental change just won't do the job. No matter how large an increment of the King's horses and of the King's men, they simply can't put Humpty Dumpty together again. The Edgar Allan Poe story, "Purloined Letter," dramatizes a situation in which incremental change fails to yield desired results, and transformational thinking becomes the preferred strategy.

In Paris, in the late 1800s, a letter was taken from the royal family's boudoir. Even though the letter's author saw the thief take it, compromising circumstances did not permit her to call attention to the misdeed. If its contents were disclosed, her honor would be stained. The thief, government Minister D., had a reputation for daring exploits. To counter such boldness, the Police Prefect was secretly called in and offered a sizeable personal reward to discreetly retrieve the letter. The Prefect determined, through a staged mugging, that the minister did not carry the purloined letter with him. A meticulous search followed for three months during the several nights each week when the minister was absent from his city apartment. Every cubic meter of space was identified, subdivided, and examined. Table legs and chair rungs were dismantled and reassembled; every book was checked page-by-page; cushions were probed with long needles—to no avail. The Prefect used the *incremental* approach, which previously served him well. Now, he wisely brought in a *transformational* thinker—detective C. Auguste Dupin (the French "Sherlock Holmes"). The two men agreed the potential for blackmail required that the letter be readily accessible to Minister D. and concluded it still resided in the thief's apartment. However, Dupin introduced a *radical new premise:* the letter wasn't found because the incremental-search strategy was inappropriate for so audacious a thief. This new premise led logically to the deduction that the letter was *not concealed*. Dupin arranged a social visit to Minister D. and saw the "hidden" letter in full view carelessly placed in a letter rack with modest changes to the envelope's appearance. On a second visit, Dupin arranged a distraction outside the minister's apartment windows that gave him time to switch envelopes. He returned the purloined letter to its grateful author. [6]

In unraveling the mystery, Dupin's transformational thinking fit the situation better than the Prefect's "let's use our tried-and-true incremental approach."

Effective leaders pose this strategic mentoring question: If you have explored a range of incremental changes that no longer stimulate your creative juices, what new premise or paradigm would help rekindle your passion?

CHOOSING A CHANGE STRATEGY

PRODUCT LIFE CYCLE S-CURVE

Leading change embraces the following two strategies:

Incremental Change	Transformational Change
◆ Remain within the current system	◆ Replace the current system
◆ Follow precedent	◆ Disrupt precedent
◆ Refine, Adjust	◆ Renew, Start over
◆ Maneuver within maze walls	◆ Knock down maze walls
◆ Produce a change in degree	◆ Produce a change in kind
◆ Create branch change	◆ Create root change
◆ Aim at continuous improvement	◆ Re-engineer through innovation

Consider incremental change when:

◆ The present system is adequate to support the desired vision and values.

◆ A backlog of cost effective, incremental change options is available.

◆ The competitive, regulatory, and technology environments in which you operate are relatively stable and predictable.

Consider transformational change when:

◆ The current system no longer yields acceptable progress toward the organization's objectives.

◆ Turbulent conditions require a fundamental change.

◆ You are prepared to address such staff resistance as concern about job security or concern about maintaining future competence in a new and unfamiliar system.

Leading Honorably Tip: Help Others Accept Change

Psychologist Kurt Lewin is known for his three-step model of change:

1. Thaw
2. Change
3. Refreeze

He suggests that leaders help others accept change by preparing them for it. This means explaining, assuring, perhaps even teaching. Converting resistance to receptivity—thawing or melting down the old to make room for the new—begins with understanding.

One way to help people achieve understanding—the thawed state—is through discussion. Consider the following questions on which to focus a discussion.

♦ What lies behind the change?

_____

_____

_____

♦ Is there any way you can make it "not happen"?

_____

_____

_____

♦ Given its seeming inevitability, what can you do about the change?

_____

_____

_____

♦ Of your choices, which is the most beneficial?

_____

_____

_____

♦ What possible benefits might evolve from the change?

_____

_____

_____

♦ Is the rate of change to come likely to increase, decrease, or remain the same?

_____

_____

_____

♦ How have we as a nation demonstrated an ability to change?

_____

_____

_____

♦ What role does technology have in facilitating or impeding change?

_____

_____

_____

♦ If more information was produced between 1965 and 1995 than was produced between 3000 B.C. and 1965 A.D., what information-adaptations do we need to make?

_____

_____

_____

◆ What can you do to lead the change rather than try to stop it?

_____

_____

_____

◆ What mistakes do people or organizations make when it comes to change?

_____

_____

_____

◆ What are possible linkages between stress and change?

_____

_____

_____

◆ What new priorities have emerged or will emerge with the (proposed) change?

_____

_____

_____

◆ What changes do you need to make to accommodate the internal changes?

_____

_____

_____

◆ What aspects of the change can you control?

_____

_____

_____

◆ What can't you control?

_____

_____

_____

◆ If you were leading the change in your organization, how would you do so?

_____

_____

_____

◆ Why do you think people cling so desperately to the past, to the familiar?

_____

_____

_____

Using Quotations to Ease Transition

Another way to facilitate discussion is with the use of quotations from notables such as these:

◆ Motivational author Napoleon Hill: "Every adversity carries with it the seed of an equivalent or greater benefit."

◆ Human behavior author Wess Roberts: "Destiny is as destiny does. If you believe you have no control, you have no control."

◆ J.C. Penney: "I am grateful for all my problems. After each one was overcome, I became stronger and more able to meet those that were still to come. I grew in all my difficulties."

Which of the sayings above could you use to help others accept the change they may be facing?

_____

_____

_____

What specifically would you say to help others transition between the old and familiar to the new and unknown?

_____

_____

_____

A Three-Way Win from the Three-Step Model of Change

Think about the winners in your carefully planned introduction to change. You, of course, will benefit—you will grow in your leadership capability. Those who have to undergo the change will benefit, for you will have lessened their fear and subsequent stress as they deal with this disruption to their normal way of doing things. And as a result of this stress reduction, all those people who come in contact with those who undergo the change (including their family members) will benefit as well.

CHAPTER 9
CREATIVITY
TOOLS

Genius is little more than
perceiving in a
non-habitual way.

—William James

*C*reativity is often shrouded in a mystical aura, as though only a few are anointed with its holy water. In reality, creativity is everyone's birthright. The leader's role is to encourage and welcome alternatives that will replace habitual patterns with something original and of value. Creative thinking starts with a subtle feeling that something is off, an itch to seek a more compelling truth, surrender for a time to not knowing.

Because creativity disrupts the familiar, leaders must be willing to risk failure, look foolish, and suffer discomfort and disorientation. Thomas Edison, after *thousands* of unsuccessful attempts to improve his primitive storage battery, asserted: "These trials were not failures. I learned more than a thousand approaches that did not work."

To be creative, you don't have to be an inventor, sculptor, physicist, writer, actor, composer, architect, or magician. Rather, you need to be curious, experimental, and willing to take on powerful people with a vested interest in maintaining the status quo. You need to reexamine past solutions currently embodied in rules, roles, and routines because formalized habits are implicit strategies for dealing with *yesterday's* concerns. One signal that an organization is at the brink of stagnation is the distribution by management of a manual on how to write manuals.

Creativity has as its domain innovation as sophisticated as nano-technology and as mundane as your breakfast bagel. (Why cut it in half before popping it into the toaster? A more creative approach may be to cut it in thirds for crisper toasting and "cutting" back on bagel calories.)

Some people are creativity naturals, but everyone can improve their "creativity quotient." Tools presented in this chapter—paradox, model-building, reframing, and metaphor—can help you see possibilities with fresh eyes or, in the words of Zen master Shunryu Suzuki, with a "beginner's mind."

Creativity Tool: Paradox

F. Scott Fitzgerald wrote: "The mark of a developed intellect is that it can accommodate two contradictory ideas at the same time." See how well you can harmonize the following disparate views.

Less Is More

An aim in art and poetry is to express truth without non-essential detail. Science uses the term "Occam's Razor" to express the "law of parsimony," which seeks the minimum number of assumptions. In turbulent times, pivotal concepts tend to be obscured by data overload. You can stimulate creativity when you apply "less-is-more" reasoning to your organizational issues. Try it.

For example, compile a list of words that might trigger ideas to improve sales or service by doing or offering *less* (rather than *more*—the conventional "wisdom.") Here are some possibilities:

Combine	Condense	Strip/Peel
Remove	Divide	Lighten
Tighten	Thin	Liquefy
Freeze	Miniaturize	Simplify
Eliminate	Eject	Dissolve
Distill	Compact	Concentrate
Separate	Reduce	Contract

Some items on this brainstorming list may trigger fresh ideas. For example, Sony captured profitable market share when it created the Walkman® by *eliminating* large speakers and *miniaturizing* electronic components. Dell Computer, after its initial launch, found that less-is-more by *eliminating* retailers in favor of direct selling; and *reducing* inventories of complete computers by assembling customized products after they were ordered. Car manufacturers *combined* functions by designing the windshield defrosting filament to also serve as a radio antenna.

Nothing Fails Like Success

An example of this paradox is the Miss America Pageant, which, launched in 1927, became the most successful television program aired in the 1950s. The pageant's enormous success encouraged producers to keep the winning formula. Young women in one-piece bathing suits and ornate evening gowns paraded before Atlantic City audiences entertaining them with their pulchritude and performing talent. During the 1960s, an era that challenged cultural norms, pageant audiences and sponsors dramatically declined. The once successful event was seen, at best, as irrelevant; at worst, insensitive to its exploitation of women as mindless sex objects.

Another example of the "success-failure-success" paradox was offered to Stanford University graduates by Steve Jobs in his June 2005 commencement address. Jobs said, "I got fired from Apple Computer very publicly. It was awful tasting medicine, but getting fired was the best thing that could have happened. It freed me to enter one of the most creative periods of my life. The heaviness of being successful was replaced by being a beginner again. I started NeXT and Pixar. In a weird turn of events, Apple bought NeXT; I returned to Apple; and Pixar went on to be the most successful animation studio in the world."

Ask yourself: Has your strategy for success (in any aspect of your life) outlived its usefulness? Has success encouraged risk-averse behavior? Examining this success/failure paradox helps you notice signs of being lulled into complacency.

More Authority Is Less Power

If you haven't the authority to conclude a deal, and need the approval of another person, you can use your lack of authority for bargaining leverage. You can truthfully say: "My manager tells me I am negotiating away more than she can approve. Can we find some middle ground acceptable to you and to her?

Here's a paradoxical quotation by Lebanese poet-philosopher, Kahlil Gibran:

And when you have reached the mountain top, then you shall begin to climb.

Recall Albert in the Chapter 1 Case Study, "The Summit," in which Albert drives himself relentlessly to reach the executive suite summit. The real top from which he could launch his climb was feeling worthy about himself. His bulldog determination to get to the top irrespective of human costs reflected

Albert's personal insecurities. To climb the leadership ladder, he needed first to gain a personal summit: his own intrinsic worthiness.

See what fresh ideas may surface for you by inquiring into these paradoxes:

Powerlessness corrupts.

You don't have time to hurry.

Be unprepared.

Expect the unexpected.

Check below the bottom line.

Take prudent risks.

It is in giving that we receive. (St. Francis)

It was the best of times; it was the worst of times. (Charles Dickens)

In addition to stimulating your creative juices, you can also have fun with paradoxical statements, such as:

I am a fanatic about moderation.

Help strikes again.

I can resist everything but temptation.
(Oscar Wilde)

Of course I believe in free will; I have no choice.
(J. B. Singer)

I can give you a definite "maybe."
(Darryl F. Zanuck)

People don't go to that restaurant anymore; it's too crowded.
(Yogi Berra)

Creativity Tool: Model Building

Another creativity tool, model building, strips a concept or activity to its bare bones and reveals crucial relationships.

As an example, consider the three states of consciousness identified by Freud. Freud's clinical terms—*superego* (internalized judge-critic), *ego* (social personality), and *id* (instinctual, impulsive, pleasure seeker) are translated in Eric Berne's model. Berne uses accessible lay language—parent, adult, child—and diagrams the functional and dysfunctional ways people communicate with one another from each state. [1]

Using an organizational context, you can see how the model shows a manager and her direct-report communicating from each of the three states of consciousness.

Manager	Employee Who Reports to Manager
<u>Adult</u>: Your recent travel expenses look high. Would you help me understand the circumstances?	<u>Adult</u>: My expenses do look high. Let me analyze them and get back to you tomorrow.
<u>Parent</u>: Your recent travel expenses are beyond belief. I want a full explanation. Our rules must be obeyed.	<u>Parent</u>: No one could have been more prudent than I. I never want to even appear to be frivolous with company funds.
<u>Child</u>: You can't even control your own spending. One more screw-up and you're history.	<u>Child</u>: I'm sorry I spent so much money. I promise not to do it again. (Later, out of earshot) She's always picking on me.

By simplifying reality, models such as Berne's help us see old patterns with fresh eyes. To construct a model, identify critical factors and how they interact. This first step is largely intuitive.

Suppose you want a model that helps you choose an effective decision making process under various circumstances. You begin by identifying two critical factors:

1. Alignment—How well aligned are the interests of the stakeholders? That is, to what degree are participants, while advancing their own interests, likely to also serve the interests of other stakeholders?

_____

_____

_____

2. Power—Who has the power to decide? That is, how is power distributed among stakeholders?

_____

_____

_____

Next, identify common decision-making processes so that you can zero in on the one that fits your situation. Possibilities:

1. You can decide alone (unilateral).
2. You can reach a decision by give-and-take bargaining with another person or party (bilateral).
3. Stakeholders can problem solve collaboratively (multilateral).

4. Stakeholders can agree to an objective criterion by which to decide (decision rule).

Which decision-making process most appropriate for your situation?

_____

_____

_____

	High Alignment	Partial Alignment
Expert Power	**unilateral** (e.g., captain orders ship evacuation)	**bilateral** (e.g., labor management bargaining)
Share Power	**multilateral** (e.g., develop a new business plan)	**decision rule** (e.g., choose company picnic date)

Relationship between alignment of interests and locus of power in reaching decisions with others.

Variables displayed in a model should illuminate attitudes and behaviors you want to better understand. They are the key to creative inquiry.

Social philosopher Charles Handy offers his views about the power of conceptual models:

> The old corporate model, which grew out of the Machine Age, is rapidly passing. It assumed the corporation is the property of its owners. Most "owners" now are investment bankers, portfolio managers, and individual stockholders. So the *property model* is outdated. Most recently, I designed a model around the concept I call the *membership community* involving mutual rights and responsibilities to enhance commitment and flexibility. [2]

Thinking with conceptual models cuts through complexity to core concerns.

Creativity Tool: Reframing

How you view a snapshot is influenced by how the photographer framed the picture. You can stimulate creative possibilities by asking yourself: If I don't accept the view of reality imposed by another person or group or by cultural conditioning, how else could I define it? Reframing looks at a situation without changing it but, rather, by changing how you understand it.

The following examples illustrate how, by reframing—changing context—you can create a reality more in harmony with your current vision and values.

> Mike Todd, Elizabeth Taylor's third husband, was a highly successful Broadway theatrical producer until he backed one show that flopped miserably. An unfriendly critic asked him, in a gloating tone of superiority, "Well, Mike, how does it feel to be poor?" Todd reframed the question, replying: "I'm not poor; I have a *cash flow* problem."

An incident involving Theodore Roosevelt also illustrates the power of reframing.

In his 1912 presidential bid, Roosevelt planned a cross-country train campaign. At each stop, he would talk to voters as his aides distributed pamphlets with his portrait on the cover. Before embarking on the trip, his campaign manager, George Perkins, discovered that the impressive photograph had imprinted below it: "Moffett Studio, Chicago." Perkins further learned, to his horror, that three million copies had been printed without consulting the copyright owner. If he paid for permission to use the photo at the going rate (up to one dollar per copy), the campaign treasury could be emptied; if he ignored the copyright question, it could become an irksome campaign issue.

Perkins creatively reframed his perception of the problem and wired Mr. Moffett:

"We plan on giving your studio national publicity as part of Mr. Roosevelt's Presidential campaign. Would you be willing to help us defray the cost of printing three million pamphlets?"

Moffett wired back: "Sorry, all I can contribute is $250."

Perkins accepted.

How would you have handled this dilemma? Yet another creative alternative would have been to buy Moffet's photography studio.

Reframing is a useful problem-solving tool. For example, imagine a new office building that opened with pomp and ceremony. But, as the building filled with tenants, complaints mounted. People were annoyed waiting for elevators even though some were designated as local, others as express to certain floors, and the system was fine tuned. Building management tried to convince occupants to stagger working hours—all to no avail. Finally, someone reframed the situation from an elevator problem to a passenger boredom problem. After mirrors were installed in the lobby, large tanks with exotic fish were displayed, and a video screen reported stock market action, elevator complaints vanished.

Here's a twist on how Mark Twain's Tom Sawyer got friends to pay for painting his picket fence by reframing their perception from painting as a distasteful chore to a pleasurable experience.

A nerdy, high-school student, Bill, was being teased by a group of classmates. To their surprise, he offered $5 to each student who devised the most creative tease. Three boys won. The following day, Bill offered $2. Again, a number of boys won. Bill kept lowering the rewards down to a nickel, at which time the teasers said:

"A nickel? Forget it!" and left Bill in peace.

Closer to home, my wife Marilyn and I were invited to India to provide management training to executives in Bombay, Bangalore, Madras, Calcutta, and New Delhi. Upon landing at Frankfurt, Germany, we were dismayed to learn of an irregularity in our visas that prevented us from boarding our flight to Bombay. From the mostly-empty Airport Sheraton (it was Christmastime), we phoned our Indian contact, who reassured us. Mr. Krishnan said each of the five seminars was fully subscribed; he would straighten out the visa misunderstanding and call us the following day at the hotel. After four days of disappointing phone calls, and waiting in the hotel ready to board a plane at a moment's notice, Marilyn and I had two options: We could blame each other about carelessness, stupidity (I had made the travel arrangements), and a missed adventure; or, we could reframe the situation.

Marilyn reframed our new perception of what appeared to be a hopeless mess as: *"God has something better in store for us."* After we had lengthy discussions with a variety of personnel at Lufthansa, they compassionately agreed to fly us virtually anywhere we wanted to go.... but that adventure is another story.

Reversing phrases sometimes generates stimulating reframing. Jesuit philosopher Teihard de Chardin reversed the conventional wisdom: "We are human beings on a spiritual journey." His reframe was more profound: "We are spiritual beings on a human journey." Another example:

The certainty of misery is preferred by some to the misery of uncertainty.

History offers this illustration of how a French army commander reframed the draconian orders he received from his superior. He was directed to quell the sporadic riots breaking out in Paris before the 1789 Revolution by shooting unarmed protesters. As his soldiers leveled their rifles, the commander shouted to the crowd: *"Mesdames et monsieurs,* I have orders to shoot the rabble. But, as I see a great number of honest, respectable citizens before me, I request that these citizens leave so that I can safely shoot the rabble." The square emptied in minutes.

Reframing helps you find fresh approaches more in harmony with values you cherish.

Creativity Tool: Metaphor

Aristotle wrote: "Ordinary words convey what we already know; it is from metaphor that we can best get hold of something fresh." For example, rather than deal with individual problems as they arise, this metaphor suggests a more comprehensive approach:

Do you want to constantly swat mosquitoes; or clean out the swamps that breed them?

While paradox invites resolution of apparent contradiction, metaphor connects two variables—concepts, objects, attitudes, activities—that share a likeness. More than poetic ornaments of language, metaphors—in connecting two dissimilar phenomena—produce a tension that generates fresh perspectives and creative possibilities.

Some metaphors are embedded so deeply in our culture that few people notice them, such as:

Time is money.

We discuss how we will "spend" our time. Employees are paid by the week; landlords receive rents monthly; dividends are distributed quarterly; budgets are approved annually. Attorneys and accountants keep track of "billable hours." Instead of unconsciously accepting metaphors that reinforce cultural norms, how might you enrich your worldview if you replaced *Time is Money* with *Time is Life*?

John Kao, Harvard Business School professor, uses the musical "jam session" to make his metaphor-as-creativity-stimulus point:

Jazz jamming is a powerful metaphor for understanding the creative process and differentiating successful companies and teams from those less successful. I use the sheet music metaphor when thinking about asset allocation. It is prescribed; it has right and wrong answers. Jamming follows jazz rules but not individual notes, giving you a different result each time. It is adaptable to new conditions. In one quick change of focus, a company can move from sheet music to jamming, and can compete faster and more creatively than its rivals. [3]

Metaphoric thinking helped DuPont find new markets for its fire-resistant fiber Nomex, which the company sold to firefighters in protective clothing. Another attractive market was aircraft interiors. However, airlines insisted that fabrics had to meet their color specifications. A daunting technical problem was the fiber's tight molecular structure that made it impervious to dyes. A DuPont scientist, who grew up in coal-mining country, compared this problem to a mine shaft where miners dig a hole in the earth and use props to keep the hole from collapsing. Using the mine-shaft metaphor, the researcher devised a way to chemically prop open holes in the Nomex structure as the material was being manufactured so it could later be filled with dyes.

To use metaphoric thinking as a leadership creativity tool, try the following exercise.

♦ Identify a concern you have such as a stalled career, marital friction, money pressures, or excessive stress.

_____

_____

_____

♦ Write a common word or phrase that may "trigger" new perspectives.

_____

_____

_____

♦ List expressions that have some connection with the word you selected.

_____

_____

_____

For example, two co-workers want to address their lack of success in collaborative problem-solving. They waste too much time and energy trying to win arguments. More helpful would be a <u>flowing</u> exchange of ideas and feelings.

Common expressions that relate to *flow*:

Water over the dam	Sink or swim
Getting into hot water	Drinking from a fire hose
Don't make waves	Out to sea
Blown out of the water	Too watered down
Boil it down	Flooded with feelings
Drowning in red ink	Sunk costs

The aim of this exercise is to find metaphoric expressions that will stimulate consideration of alternative behaviors. For example, the co-workers in this situation may be so *flooded with feelings* they *bottle* them up, preferring the *safe harbor* of impersonal argument. Or, rather than a *deluge* of data, they need a *pool* of information.

Two linguistic philosophers, George Lakoff and Mark Johnson, find:

"An experience can only be fully comprehended using other kinds of entities and experiences—that is, in terms of metaphor.... We [George and Mark] still react with awe when we notice ourselves living by metaphors like "*Love is a journey.*"[4]

Metaphor can touch tender places in oneself, such as evoked by this poem-song excerpt, "The Rose," by Amanda McBroom.[5]

**Some say love, it is a *river* that drowns the
tender reed Some say love, it is a *razor*
that leaves your soul to bleed
Some say love, it is a *hunger*, an endless aching need
I say love, it is a *flower* and you its only seed.**

Metaphor can also be used to introduce a light touch, such as: "When I am constrained to report my team's progress at meetings using only a sound bite summary, I feel like someone who has to perform a ballet in a telephone booth."

Or, you might metaphorically observe: "Education, like a manual on how to have good sex, is improved by experiential learning."

The thread that runs through the four creativity tools covered in this chapter—paradox, model-building, reframing, and metaphor—is that they all impose a *constraint*. When I wrote a monthly magazine column, I was instructed by the editor to "kill widows." (Killing widows is not a bloody affair; it is journalistic jargon for eliminating single words that appear at the end of a paragraph to conserve magazine space.) Invariably, as a result of this constraint, my re-writing resulted in clearer phrasing and more creative expression.

Exercise in Creativity

To see for yourself how constraint spurs creativity, try this exercise: List objects that are all *white*. Stop after two minutes.

_____

_____

_____

_____

_____

_____

Now, add a second constraint: Add to your list those objects that are both *white* and also are *edible*.

_____

_____

_____

_____

_____

Did your creativity expand when you added the second constraint such as marshmallows, sweet cream, sour cream, cream cheese, whipped cream, milk, cooked egg white, rice, salt, sugar?

Creativity—paradoxically—thrives on constraint. It also thrives on an ever-present openness to curiosity and, as Emily Dickinson wrote: "I dwell in possibility."

Leading Honorably Tip: Make Creative Applications

To lead is to create a new set of circumstances—not just for the sake of having something new but because a new set of circumstances will improve a situation. Leaders take chances when they create something new. If you are creating, you know you encounter some risk when you move from the old to the new-and-improved. If you are not creating new circumstances, you may need to assess what is holding you back. Compare your typical actions to the actions that creative people take by assessing yourself according to the following descriptions.

Ascertain Your Creativity Quotient

Do you have what it takes for "create-ability"? Here is a way to find out. The following list contains the traits of highly creative individuals. For each, score yourself along this continuum:

1 = Not at all true of me

2 = Somewhat true of me

3 = Often true of me

4 = Completely true of me

Traits

1.	Can tolerate confusion	_____
2.	Is willing to explore	_____
3.	Is receptive to new ideas	_____
4.	Sees the invisible	_____
5.	Sees problems as opportunities	_____
6.	Is self-directed	_____
7.	Can defer judgment	_____
8.	Concentrates well	_____
9.	Thinks divergently	_____
10.	Has a child's mind	_____
11.	Is not limited by restraints	_____
12.	Sees the big picture	_____
13.	Copes well with rejection	_____
14.	Is persistent	_____
15.	Is self-confident	_____

16.	Is patient with ideas	_____
17.	Is resourceful	_____
18.	Is entrepreneurial	_____
19.	Dislikes routine	_____
20.	Can juggle tasks	_____
21.	Thinks fluidly	_____
22.	Thinks innovatively	_____
23.	Uses metaphors	_____
24.	Probes ideas deeply	_____
25.	Can bravely defy the norm	_____
Total:	Your Assessment Number	_____

A score of 80 or higher suggests you are indeed one who can "see" the change that is needed and then work to create it so that many parties will benefit. If your score was in the 70s or lower, do not despair. For each item that you rated a "1" or "2," you can take action to raise that score. How? One of the best ways is to ask a friend, colleague, or professional coach to provide feedback about your efforts to improve in a particular area.

CHAPTER 10
CRITERIA-BASED LEADERSHIP

The highest wisdom
has but one science—
the science of the
whole.

—Leo Tolstoy

*C*riteria-based leadership uses mutiple lenses to see the whole. When dealing with proposals, plans, and performance, seven criteria offer a comprehensive overview by which to focus leadership conversations.

These pivotal criteria are:

◆ technical

◆ economic

◆ ethical/legal

◆ environmental

◆ social-psychological

◆ political

◆ spiritual

***Technical:* Will the proposed plan work? Can it be accomplished in the desired timeframe?**

The technical criterion focuses on performance goals. For example, can automobile manufacturers build vehicles that meet targets for fuel efficiency, emissions, safety, power, handling, quiet, and dependability? When? Can semi-floating condos be built in the ocean off California's coast? Is a cure likely for Parkinson's Disease based on stem-cell research? The technical criterion can be applied to sophisticated issues, like tracking satellites, or mundane operations, like hand-packing sardines on an assembly line.

Economic: **What are the financial risks? Is the proposal fiscally viable? Is accounting information accurate and complete?**

This criterion assesses likely costs, probable return on investment, and level of uncertainty—all entrepreneurial risk-taking judgments. Combining the technical and economic criteria poses the question: "Is it cost effective?"

Ethical/Legal: **Is the proposed action fair, lawful, and safe? Is it right?**

Particularly in the light of corporate scandals—from insider trading, to "cooking the books," to executives treating corporate asset accounts like personal piggy banks—the ethical criterion deserves organization-wide attention.

During a single day, *The Wall Street Journal* reported these breaches of ethics and law:

1. The former Worldcom company's controller admitting to "going along with false accounting entries that eventually became part of an 11 billion dollar fraud."

2. A Florida judge wrote that she would tell the jury that Morgan Stanley "had a role in helping appliance maker Sunbeam Corporation conceal accounting woes."

3. "AIG fired two executives who chose not to answers investigators' questions on Fifth Amendment grounds."

4. "Adelphia is close to an agreement to pay $725 million to settle claims from its corporate looting and accounting scandals."

Leaders can gain insight into ethical behavior from the work of Lawrence Kohlberg, who headed Harvard's Center for Moral Development. He designed a three-level model of ethical reasoning with each level reflecting more developed moral maturity.[1]

At *Level One*, the focus is on *punishment avoidance* and *reciprocity*. Will a proposed action be rewarded or punished? Is a proposed exchange equitable? Is it okay to have a social phone conversation during business hours, or check your stock portfolio prices on the Internet because you will be working late? If you do me a favor, will I owe you a favor in return? Level One is concerned with personal consequences.

Level Two aims at *maintaining systems* that are fair and contribute to societal *well-being*. You obey traffic laws and refrain from going through a red light late at night even though no police are around; your company sets up a phone number for reporting manager misconduct; you prepare children for school in accordance with prescribed dress codes. At this level of moral reasoning, behavior is guided by social norms.

At *Level Three*, the *universal principles* level, and most evolved form of ethical reasoning, you are willing to make personal sacrifices to advance the greatest good for the greatest number. Exemplars are Mahatma Gandhi and Martin Luther King, Jr.—two men who dedicated themselves to life-affirming principles and who both suffered the ultimate price. Gandhi's words reflect this level of reasoning: "I disregarded the order of the British magistrate not for want of respect, but in obedience to the higher law of our being, the voice of conscience."[2]

To see how Kohlberg's model can be applied, consider the experience of my friend Hal who fought in the "Battle of the Bulge," Germany's last big World War II offensive. During close quarters fighting, three of Hal's comrades were taken prisoner and killed. As the tide of battle turned, Hal's squad took several German prisoners. His platoon sergeant, bent on revenge, ordered Hal to take the prisoners to a deserted barn and shoot them. An eighteen-year-old private at the time, Hal refused to follow the order.

Hal's reaction to the sergeant's direct command can be understood in terms of Kohlberg's model.

- *Level One.* Hal could have followed orders to shoot prisoners and justified his action based on *reciprocity*—"I am doing to them exactly what they did to us."

- *Level Two.* If Hal were to appear at a court martial for disobedience, he could defend his action as congruent with *maintaining a just system* under international law that decrees prisoners-of-war may not be killed except attempting escape.

- *Level Three.* Hal could have reasoned (as he did) that murdering defenseless people is inhuman. He could have been reassured by Ralph Waldo Emerson's words: "Nothing can bring you peace but the triumph of *principles*." (His sergeant didn't bring charges against Hal, who was later wounded, sent home, and currently practices law in Los Angeles.)

Environmental: Will the action under consideration result in changes that are ecologically benign, sustainable, and aesthetic?

Ecologist Garrett Hardin dramatized the need for environmentally wise thinking with his "tragedy of the commons" metaphor.[3] Hardin asks us to imagine one hundred farmers each grazing one cow in the commons (central community pasture). As farmers add a second and third cow to gain individual economic advantage, at some point, the added grazing is no longer sustainable, resulting in a grassless, muddy field that makes everyone a loser.

It is not a stretch to appreciate the connection between violating a lush commons and cutting trees at an unsustainable rate or whaling without restraint. The leadership enigma lies in resolving the temptation of individuals to reap short-term gains (where "short term" may be decades) while future generations suffer long-term consequences.

One approach to overcoming the lure of personal advantage is to create a community with shared common interests, a sense of belonging, and a personal stake in the consequences of everyone's behavior. Social psychologist David Myers tells of his experience with community conservation.

"On the Puget Sound island where I grew up, our small neighborhood shared a communal water supply. On hot summer days when our reservoir ran low, a light came on signaling our fifteen families to conserve. Recognizing our responsibility to one another, and feeling that our conservation really counted, the reservoir never ran dry." [4]

The environmental imperative to overcome individual (or corporate) gratification at community expense is a challenge now as it was over a century ago when Chekhov wrote:

"Man has been endowed with reason and with power to create. But up to now he has been a destroyer. Forests keep disappearing, rivers dry up, wild life's become extinct, the climate is ruined, and the land grows poorer and uglier every day." [5]

His contemporary sounding words were prophetic and sobering. Cold reason itself is not enough; compassion for future generations is crucial.

Power and Political Influence: **Will others join you with needed resources and support?**

Power and influence over others is sought by people as disparate as family members, corporate executives, and tribal warlords. It is a hollow goal. Except in crises, where speed is crucial, unilateral top-down power invites countervailing power—resistance, cover-up, and manipulation. It fails to stir creativity, fails to integrate diverse perspectives, and fails to enlist consistent support. As pioneering management consultant Mary Parker Follett wrote in the early 1900s:

The central problem of social relations is power. Our task is not where to place power, but how to develop it. Genuine power is coactive—the fruitful uniting of individual contributions. [6]

While Follett's definition of coactive power is identical to *leadership* as expressed in this book, the usual context of power is not inclusive, and not based on the shared wisdom of conversation. Rather, in conventional use, power derives from position, expertise, wealth, charisma, the capacity to limit another's options, and the concealing of "privileged" information.

An illustration of how power can be exercised abusively, based on withholding information, is described with the wry humor of this Garrison Keillor story.

Gladys just stepped out of her shower when the doorbell rang. Wrapping herself in a large towel, and knowing her husband was working in the basement, she opened the back door. A well-dressed stranger asked for driving directions and added, "Please forgive me for being so forward, but may I say how beautiful you are?" He went on: "I feel hesitant to ask this, but would you be willing to accept $300 to drop your towel?" Gladys remembered a dress she wanted

to buy and dropped her towel. The stranger gave her cash with a final request. "For another $100 would you turn once slowly? She reasoned, "I've gone this far, why not?" As the man drove off and Gladys stepped back into the kitchen, her husband called: "Whose car just drove away?" "Don't know. He was about your height, your age, balding, and drove a white Lincoln Town Car. "I wish you had told me," her husband called from the basement, "that was my cousin from Chicago. He phoned yesterday to say he was passing through and would stop to repay the $400 he borrowed from me." [7]

Social/Psychological: Will the proposed action nurture personal growth and relationships that support mutual satisfaction, trust, and a commitment to common objectives?

The essence of leadership is the capacity to inspire commitment from individuals and teams. Its crux is building trust by telling the truth, disclosing what is relevant, and delivering on promises. The social/psychological criterion focuses on empathic connection between people that energizes them to plan and work together toward common goals. Supportive leadership provides respect and appreciation that encourages others to make the best contributions of which they are capable.

Spiritual: Will the proposed action promote a sense of unity, and honor what is eternal in all people?

Not every action plan will directly address a significant spiritual concern—even when spirituality is broadly defined as the unifying influence that transcends all material gain. At times, however, we know that how we act transcends "ordinary" behavior. Take, for example, an event my wife experienced as a child.

> When she was four, Marilyn, her mother, and two-year-old brother were spending two weeks at a Catskill Mountain hotel to escape the oppressive New York City heat. One evening as all three were asleep, their bedroom door burst open. A young bellboy—perhaps on the very first job he ever held—and Marilyn's aunt screamed "Wake up! Wake up! The building's on fire!" The bellboy grabbed Marilyn and ran to the staircase only to see it collapse, engulfed in flame. They darted to the only remaining exit and all breathlessly reached safety minutes before the entire building imploded into charred rubble.

Why did a minimum wage bellboy risk a horrible incendiary death to save total strangers? Something within impelled his selfless action—an instinctive valuing of human life coupled with courage and generosity of spirit—core qualities that are the essence of leadership.

Case Study: The Trusted Employee

Mary   Head bookkeeper, reports to Erwin King

Erwin King   Controller, reports to company president

Tim   Sales manager

Vicki, Doris   Clerks

The following action takes place at the corporate headquarters of an organization with about 400 employees.

Tim visits Mary in her office to get a travel advance.

MARY: You know the rules, Tim. No cash advance for a trip until you turn in your expense report for the last one.

TIM: Mary, I'd love to. But my plane leaves in less than an hour. C'mon, if Erwin hassles you about it, I'll take the heat.

MARY: Okay. But I want both reports the day you get back. [Mary begins counting cash into Tim's palm.] Three hundred, three-fifty, four hundred. Please sign here for the cash advance.

TIM: [puts the cash in his wallet and picks up his bags.] Gotta run. Is your mother any better?

MARY: About the same. But at least she's home now. Thanks for asking, Tim.

[Two clerks, Vicki and Doris, enter. The wall clock reads 8:40 as they quickly go to their desks.]

VICKI: Mr. King's not in yet, is he?

MARY: He's been in for half an hour. When he says 8:30, he means at your desk and working—not just arriving at work.

DORIS: The salespeople come and go whenever they feel like it.

MARY: You know they travel and work late hours.

DORIS: Show up early, work late. Is that how you made it from clerk to head bookkeeper?

MARY: Well, it didn't hurt. Doris, do you have last month's expense reports and cash advance records? I can't find them.

DORIS: Mr. King took them out of the file yesterday.

ERWIN KING [from the doorway of his office]:Mary, will you step in here for a moment?

MARY: Right away, Mr. King.

ERWIN [to Mary as she enters and closes the door]: Please have a seat. As you know, Price Waterhouse Coopers comes in next week for their half-year audit, and...

MARY: If you are concerned about Tim's overdue expense report, I just spoke with him this morning. He knows that Thursday is the absolute deadline.

ERWIN: Actually, I'm more concerned about other expense reports. Mary, you've worked for me enough years to know what a stickler I am for expense reporting. And, that my first rule is that they have to be done in ink.

MARY: I keep after them, Mr. King, but lately...

ERWIN: There are four or five examples here of questionable erasures, mostly for cash advances. Ring any bells?

MARY [quickly, looking away]: No.

[As they stare at each other for a moment, Mary fights back her tears admitting...

Yes.... it rings a lot of bells. My mother's first hospital stay was a financial disaster for me. But this last one wiped me out. I borrowed to the limit from banks, relatives, even friends. I was still short of what I needed to pay the hospital.

ERWIN: So your answer was dipping into petty cash?

MARY: Yes.

ERWIN: How much?

MARY: Exactly seven hundred dollars. I planned to replace it, a hundred a month until it was all paid back.... I know you're disappointed.

ERWIN:Shocked is more like it. You paid your dues here, studied evenings, moved up to head our bookkeeping unit. You've been the model of how our employees should perform…up to this point.

MARY: It won't happen again.

ERWIN:This is extremely serious. I can't ignore it. Mary, you violated the basic trust a controller has to have in a bookkeeper.

MARY [obviously contrite]: I'll earn that trust back, you'll see….

ERWIN:My inclination, frankly, is dismissal. But in view of your hard work and loyalty for over seven years, I'll talk with the president before I make a decision. Don't discuss our conversation with anyone. I'll let you know in the morning.

MARY [as she leaves Erwin's office]:Yes sir.

If *you* were president of this organization, when Erwin asked for your views, what would you say to him?

_____

_____

_____

_____

_____

Case Study Discussion

Let's get clarity on exactly what happened and what we can learn from this situation. Our twin objectives are to have *trustworthy employees*, and an *effective, reliable system* for handling employee travel funds. At this point, we are satisfying neither objective. Let's apply the *multiple criteria* approach to help us focus on how to deal with Mary's transgression and how to improve our cash advance system.

Note: At leadership workshops, participants tend to focus exclusive attention on what to do with Mary. Did you? I recall an extreme example in which a participant simply said: "I don't need to discuss this one. Fire Mary's ass! What's the next case?"

What is so helpful about looking at real situations via case studies is the opportunity to see one's tendency to quickly converge on a solution. Viewing the problem situation through multiple-criteria lenses stimulates creative possibilities and opens the opportunity to learn from each experience.

Technical Criterion

A tamper-resistant system is needed. It could require two signatures to assure money-handling integrity. Alternatively, a new system could be developed, such as issuing plastic credit cards for business travel. In the "Mary situation," the truth of Mary's story should be verified by checking hospital receipts and checking for expense report erasures over the time period of Mary's tenure as head bookkeeper.

Economic Criterion

Not only would credit cards for travelers be inexpensive, they would provide a neutral, third-party audit trail. Other economic questions stimulated by this case: Should the company have a loan policy for employees with emergency needs? Should the company join a credit union where loans could be made available to employees without company involvement? Are compensation policies fair, current, and periodically reviewed? Should the company design a plan that allows employees to purchase health insurance benefits for elderly parents at employee group rates?

Legal/Ethical Criterion

Mary has committed an act of criminal embezzlement. In general, embezzlement is an under-reported crime because it is a source of embarrassment to management. Does this company have a responsibility to prosecute Mary in court? If the facts as portrayed by Mary prove true, criminal prosecution would be an excessive punishment. In any event, the company's attorneys should be consulted before any action is taken. For example, is Mary bonded? If so, what are the implications?

Political Criterion

As president of this company, you may want to take a few minutes at your next Board of Directors meeting to mention the Mary situation. You might say that you have consulted your auditor for suggestions that are being implemented. Your proactive stance in briefly discussing the topic would preclude future surprises, such as Board members later reading a newspaper item headlined: *"ABC Company sacks distraught bookkeeper while her mother is dying of cancer."*

Social-Psychological Criterion

Why was Erwin so aloof from Mary that he seemed uninformed about the family pressure she was under? Maybe he could benefit from some interpersonal communication mentoring. To help support employees experiencing trying times in their lives, the company should also consider instituting an Employee Assistance Program. Professionals in these programs are available to offer confidential counseling to employees with issues involving emotional concerns, addiction problems, and financial difficulties.

A general question Erwin and the president should explore is why it took a crisis for them to examine how their operations could be improved.

Leading Honorably Tip: Establish Guiding Principles

Just as a mission is the overarching frame of reference for a team's ultimate accomplishment, guiding principles serve as the overarching frame of reference for the team's day-by-day operation. These ground rules will see the team through to successful completion of their project.

Research shows that the ideal team has seven or eight members, although, of course, size is no guarantee of success or failure. Teams operate best under the guidance of a leader who:

◆ Involves all members

◆ Is familiar with members' talents

◆ Knows how to manage conflict (not eliminate it)

◆ Understands team dynamics

◆ Periodically assesses the team's success

Such a leader is also dedicated to the team's mission and knows how to inspire without pushing, obtain approval without fawning, and celebrate without gloating. These are the traits of an honorable leader.

Ideally, a leader's followers are committed, contributing, cooperative team members who believe in the organization's mission and are determined to fulfill it. (Passion goes a long way toward making great things happen.) Ground rules help ensure that all team members respect everyone's time and one another.

The Winner's Circle

You will be expected to create a set of ground rules for the next leadership project you take on. Who will emerge as winners from your establishing these guiding principles?

Certainly your team will, for they will have clarity of purpose. Future teams will be winners as well, for you will have "taught" your team members a critical aspect of successful leadership. Those members are bound to ensure such clarity of purpose guides future teams on which they serve. And the immediate winners will be those affected—positively—by the change your leadership will put into place.

CONCLUSION

In Conclusion

Leadership mastery expresses itself in many forms. Leaders help us transcend what we believe to be our limitations. They seed constructive change. They help us dissolve rigidities, access our inner wisdom, and connect with others in ways that invite generous, authentic sharing.

In the process of leading, here are the key concerns leaders must address with other stakeholders.

Set Intention

- Define the problem or opportunity that warrants attention.
- Clarify current reality and the underlying need for change.
- Specify important constraints (values, budget, timeframe).
- Share hoped-for outcomes and leadership commitment.

Plan

- Invite stakeholders to planning conversations.
- Gather relevant information.
- Identify incremental and transformational change opportunities.

- Evaluate change possibilities against applicable criteria: technical, economic, ethical/legal, environmental, social-psychological, political, and spiritual.
- Consider small-scale trials or gradual phase-in to reduce risk.

Implement and Follow-up

- Address resistance to planned changes.
- Acquire needed support and resources.
- Monitor progress. Reinforce what works; change what doesn't.
- Reflect on lessons learned.

Leaders help us transcend what we believe are our limits. They seed constructive change without the need to impose their will. May your leadership adventure be satisfying and productive as you travel the path opened by a curious mind and compassionate heart.

NOTES

Notes

Chapter 1. The Introspective Leader

1. Ralph Stayer, "How I learned to let my workers lead"
   Harvard Business Review, November–December, 1990.

2. N. Kazantzakis, *Zorba The Greek*, New York: Touch-
   stone, 1952.

3. The expression, "God doesn't make junk," is used by
   leaders of the "Marriage Encounter" experience.

Chapter 2. Where Is the Truth?

1. Jack Welsh is quoted in Robert B. Shaw, *Trust in the Balance*, San Francisco, Jossey-Bass, p. 164.

2. T. S. Eliot, *Selected Poems*, "The Love Song of J. Alfred
   Prufrock," London: Farber & Farber, 1938.

Chapter 3. How You Know

1. Harold J. Leavitt, "Beyond the Analytic Manager," *California Management Review*, Summer, 1975.

2. Julia Cameron, *The Artist's Way*, New York: Putnam,
   1992, pp. 12–13.

3. Alan W. Watts, *The Wisdom of Insecurity*, New York: Pantheon, 1951, p. 56.

4. *The Economist*, June 12, 2004, p.13.

5. Carlos Eire, Interview on PBS *News Hour with Jim Lehrer*, November 25, 2003.

6. Frances Vaughn, *Awakening Intuition*, New York: Anchor Books, 1979, p. 122.

7. Patricia Garfield, *Creative Dreaming*, New York: Simon & Schuster, 1995, pp. 70–71.

8. Philip Goldberg, *The Intuitive Edge*, Boston: Houghton Mifflin, 1982, p. 148.

9. Frances Vaughan, *Awakening Intuition*, p. 121.

10. Ibid, p. 137.

11. Robert McKee, "Storytelling That Moves People," *Harvard Business Review*, June, 2003, p. 52.

12. Donald B. Calne, *Within Reason*, New York: Pantheon, 1999, p. 6.

13. Michael McCaskey, *The Executive Challenge*, Boston: Pitman, 1982., p. 115.

14. M. Mangalindan, "The Grown-up at Google," *Wall Street Journal*, April 22, 2004.

15. Philip Gourevitch, "A Cold Case," *The New Yorker*, February 14, 2000, p. 42.

16. Eugene Gendlin, *Focusing*, New York: Bantam, 1997.

Chapter 4. Managing Stress

1. S. I. Hayakawa, *Symbol, Status and Personality*, N. Y.: Harcourt, Brace and World. 1953.

Chapter 5. The Leadership Conversation

1. Early NTL Institute and Tavistock communication training is described in Kenneth Beane, Leland Bradford, Jack Gibb and Ronald Lippitt, eds., *The Laboratory Method of Changing and Learning*, Palo Alto, Calif.: Science & Behavior Books, 1975.

2. Charles Handy interview in *Thought Leaders*, Joel Kurtzman, ed., San Francisco: Jossey-Bass, 1998, p. 6.

3. Ram Das, *Still Here*, New York: Penguin, 2000, p. 130.

Chapter 6. Dealing with Disagreement

1. D. N. Perkins, *The Mind's Best Work*, Cambridge: Harvard University Press, 1981

2. Herb Kindler, *Managing Conflict*, 3rd. Ed., Boston, Thomson Learning, 1996.

3. Gabriel Garcia Marquez, *Love in the Time of Cholera*, New York: Penguin, 1996.

4. Dumas Malone, *Jefferson and His Time*, Vol. 1, University of Virginia Press, 1948, p. 409.

Chapter 7. Taking Risks

1. Kenneth MacCrimmon and Donald Wehrung, *Taking Risks: The Management of Uncertainty*, New York: The Free Press, 1986, pp. 18–19.

2. For historical examples of poorly conceived risk taking, see Barbara Tuchman, *The March of Folly*, New York: Ballantine Books, 1984.

3. David Garvin, "Building A Learning Organization," *Harvard Business Review*, July-August, 1993, p. 85.

Chapter 8. Leading Change

1. Derek de Solla Price, *Science Since Babylon*, New Haven: Yale University Press, 1961, p.125.

2. Joseph Ratner, Ed., *Intelligence in the Modern World: John Dewey's Philosophy*, New York: Modern Library, 1939, p. vi.

3. James Baldwin, *Nobody Knows My Name*, New York: Vintage, 1992.

4. Indries Shah, *Tales of the Dervishes*, London: Jonathan Cape, 1967, p. 12.

5. Charles E. Lindblom, "The Science of Muddling Through," *Public Administration Review*, 1959, 19(2), pp. 78–88.

6. Edgar Allen Poe, *Great Tales and Poems*, New York: Washington Square Press, 1940, pp. 199–219.

Chapter 9. Creativity Tools

1. Eric Berne, *Games People Play*, New York, Ballantine, 1964. The model was refined by Thomas A, Harris in *I'm OK—You're OK*, New York: Avon, 1967.

2. Charles Handy interview in *Thought Leaders*, Joel Kurtzman, ed., San Francisco: Jossey-Bass, 1998, p.6.

3. John Kao interview in *Thought Leaders*, Joel Kurtzman, ed., San Francisco: Jossey-Bass, 1998, p. 54.

4. George Lakoff and Mark Johnson, *Metaphors We Live By*, Chicago: University of Chicago Press, p. 239.

5. Amanda McBroom, "The Rose," recorded in her album, *Portraits.*

Chapter 10. Criteria-Based Leadership

1. Lawrence Kohlberg, "Moral Thinking," *Psychology Today*, February, 1979, pp. 48–92.

2. *Mohandas Gandhi, An Autobiography*, Boston: Beacon Press, 1957, p.414.

3. Garrett Hardin, "The Tragedy of the Commons," *Science*, Vol. 162, 1968, pp. 519–521.

4. David G. Myers, *Social Psychology*, New York: McGraw-Hill, 1999, p.522.

5. Anton Chekov's *Uncle Vanya*, first performed in 1899.

6. M. P. Follett, *Creative Experience*, London: Longmans, Green & Co., 1924, p. viii.

7. Garrison Keillor, Broadcast on his weekly radio program, "Prairie Home Companion" on April 7, 2001.

INDEX

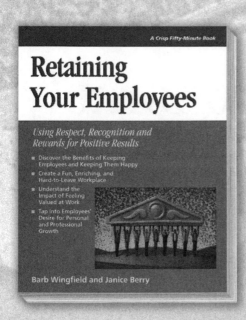

Retaining Your Employees

By Barb Wingfield and Janice Berry

Book $13.95 U.S., ISBN: 1-56052-607-6
Instructor Guide $100.00 U.S., ISBN: 1-4188-1485-7

Companies of all sizes are finding an urgent new priority—keeping employees. This book takes you through the critical ideas of employee retention using the Three Rs—Respect, Recognition, and Rewards—as the basis for any program designed to keep people around. It also serves as a comprehensive guide to supervisory skills.

Check out more Fifty-Minute™ Guides: